IN OCEANS DEEP

Redemptive Suffering
and the
Crucified God

Eduardo J. Echeverria

lec✝io
Lectio Publishing, LLC
Hobe Sound, Florida, USA

www.lectiopublishing.com

All translations, unless otherwise noted, are those of the author.

Foreword by Genevieve Deely
Photographs of Penny Deely by John Deely

Edited by Eric Wolf

ISBN 978-1-943901-07-4
Library of Congress Control Number: 2018932666

Published by Lectio Publishing, LLC
Hobe Sound, Florida 33455
www.lectiopublishing.com

In Memory of My Beloved Granddaughter
Penelope Grace Deely (2014-2016)

With Gratitude for John and Genevieve Deely

And full of joy at a new beginning:
Hope Elizabeth Deely, October 8, 2017

They grieved but not without hope. (1 Thess 4:13)

Foreword

"Without the cross of Jesus and his resurrection, my grief would be without hope." (1 Thess 4:13)

My Dad, Eduardo Echeverria, asked me whether I would consider writing the Foreword to his book on Christ and suffering. At first I was reluctant because I was so caught up in the whirlwind of my own suffering, that I wasn't sure whether I could articulate my grief, and even if I could, would it be helpful to others dealing with grief, particularly as a result of losing a beloved child? However, as time has gone on—it was one year last September 25 since we lost our precious Penelope Grace—I have been inspired to write out my thoughts and have found this expression to be cathartic.

The past year has been a journey on the worst of turbulent seas for my husband John and me, but we both agreed early on, we do not want our loss to define the rest of our lives. It is very important to us that we still celebrate life's goodness, of course while still living authentically. I do believe it is that decision we made together, with trust in God, that has opened the door to some incredible experiences and healing.

We are by no means "over" this loss, as that is not possible. But we are learning to thrive with the sadness, little by little. October 8, 2017, we received the gift of our second daughter, Hope Elizabeth Deely. To be able to parent another child, Penelope's little sister, is by far the biggest gift John and I could ever have received from our loving Father.

Below are some journal entries that I felt compelled to share on social media. I did so to let our loved ones know how we are doing and to speak truth in our rediscovering of God's love for us. There is no particular order in terms of state of mind and heart. They are true to the nature of grief, with its lack of linear structure or care for any stages of the grieving process.

12/1/16

My Dear Depression, Yes I refer to you as dear. You are not the dark night of the soul about which so many tell me. You are only disguised as this. Under the staggering layers of anxiety, migraines, lack of desire to eat or socialize, under the mountainous weight you burden each of my limbs with, is a little white furry bunny. So soft and so pure, only wanting to help me through. You hop between the green pastures of my heart and my mind, stopping to let me pet you, hold you. Those moments of petting...oh those painful, ocean tear-filled, torturous moments...sometimes they last for a minute and sometimes for days. I realize, I must welcome you. You turn off my world, I am forced to stop, to pet you. Eventually, you'll hop off into the distance. Even though you overstayed your welcome, I say thank you, and also, I hope never to see you again.

12/5/16

I've had a really difficult time the last few days with my grief manifesting itself in panic attacks and extreme vulnerability and feelings of fear. My Dad texted me this prayer today, and I found it comforting. The Blessed Mother Mary is significant because she not only shares the grief of losing her child, but she represents the sacred love that can be born in all of us, men and women. So much love to you all, especially my neighbors this week.

> REMEMBER, O most gracious Virgin Mary, that never was it known that anyone who fled to thy protection, implored thy help, or sought thy intercession was left unaided. Inspired with this confidence, I fly to thee, O Virgin of virgins, my Mother; to thee do I come; before thee I stand, sinful and sorrowful. O Mother of the Word Incarnate, despise not my petitions, but in thy mercy hear and answer me. Amen.

1/24/16

The power in your mind is activated by faith. I was thinking how I'm reluctant to accept the possibility of joy; not because I don't want it, oh I really, really do, but more so because I just don't understand how could I ever feel joy again? I look at a photo of my baby dancing and hugging her sweet Daddy and it crushes me...not my soul, not my spirit, but my heart. It literally feels torn into a thousand pieces.

3/5/17

While I was sleeping, early this morning an angel whispered these words into my ears:

Hold onto those good memories,
The bad ones we tuck away and forget.
Those memories are proof that a love exists.
And be sure to make new good memories,
So that those who love you, have something to hold onto,
When the time comes for you to return Home.

4/28/17

It was Penny's third birthday yesterday—the second worst day of my life. I wish I could post a message of hope and faith but it's just not in me. My heart, my throat, my eyes, my stomach, actually my entire body, ache from the tears...from the pain of not being able to walk into our Penny's room and sing *Happy Birthday* as we did for the two years before, with her Daddy playing the ukulele, while we watched her green eyes light up with excitement. We don't get to do that ever again with our most precious Penny. I feel so angry and so very sad that this happened. I just don't understand. So much advice given to us that we "accept, because it will be easier that way." But no, there is no acceptance at this point. Seven months in and I am still very much not OK with being unable to kiss her, hear her sing, and talk to me all day long. We have been robbed of so many experiences with our daughter who constantly evoked in us love, laughter, light, silly thoughts, as well as such profound ones.

5/15/17

I so badly want to feel like my old self —innocent, happy and so full of joy with the will to create as an actor. But I've been struggling. And I mean on the most basic level, I mean to just survive. Seven and a half months ago my beautiful two-and-a-half-year-old Penelope Grace lost her life to meningitis within 24 hours. She woke up singing in her crib as she always did on Friday September 23, and by early Sunday morning, September 25, my husband and I were saying goodbye to our beloved daughter. As parents this is the most shattering, holy experience—yet a relieving one too. Most of our precious daughter's vital organs had not survived the disease and should they have by some miracle, sadly her brain had not. My brilliant, wise, gentle, loving, musical, funny, joyful daughter who carried a magnificent light would be a silent, immobile shell. We couldn't fathom this existence for her, and so knowing she would be safe, whole and loved by God, we entrusted her to his loving hands.

However, this is not a letter about her passing, it is about the will to survive—the most basic level of creating. I don't want to die although I have thought about it a few times. My life seemed to stop when her life did. My heart seemed to stop when her life did. And yet here I am, plodding along every day. How?

Most definitely we have an army of loving support from family and friends and even strangers. But there is a powerful ingredient that one only needs just a pinch of, and needs not a trip to the store for, nor ever runs out if we are open to its working power in us. It is the grace of God we are all gifted with. That grace is a light within us that is our source. Sometimes it's just a tiny flicker, and sometimes it's burning so bright that in its presence, others know and feel it immediately.

We were born to follow the instruction of God, the master of creation, who only has one rule, and that is to love. It is our choice and it is no simple task, but should we follow, oh the joy we can experience! You might say to yourself, I can't. I don't have the strength. Just let me be. Leave me alone. I'd rather die. And to this I say, I understand. But just know, without us even participating, we were born with an engine programmed to love. The word love is just a romantic word for create. God has broken off a piece of His body, for each and every one of us, thus no one is more special than the other, and all of us are special because we are created in His image. This piece, in the form of our spirit can never die—it's an energy that stands strong beyond trauma, beyond sorrow, beyond relationship malfunction, beyond violent abuse, and most powerfully, beyond death.

My sweet daughter Penny continues to live, to create, to love, sending herself to her loved ones in all sorts of imaginative ways. And I lean deep into those gifts. And because love is contagious, when I lean in, I feel hope, the kindling of my light, and the will to live, the will to create takes one tiny step closer to my heart. There will come a day when I feel more of my joyful self. Right now it is OK to grieve, to feel the intense pain and sorrow, as I do daily, and for as long as I need to, because I am trusting that gift from God, my inner light, is programmed for thriving. That is the thought I leave with you creators—no matter what is happening in your life, God lives within you and you can rest knowing you are not doing this life alone.

5/25/17

I've been experiencing so many realizations in terms of what we have lost with the passing of our Penny girl. So many big moments, and so many little moments in our daughter's life. I still remember the butterfly feelings of excitement at Penny learning how to clap, watching her hilarious and disapproving face when she tried solids for the first time at six months, when she understood and could say her name was Penelope Grace Deely, or how she could spell Penny—"P-e-n-n-yyyyy" with a huge smile. The list goes on and on, and on. It's so very sad, and so very deeply disappointing that the excitement so abruptly and shockingly stopped at two and a half years old. Possibly it's why it's so painful to be around other toddlers, being reminded so acutely how your baby didn't get that chance to grow and what you are missing out on. Of course I am glad for these children, as they are doing what they are meant to be doing, growing up. Although I'd prefer to always focus on the future in a positive light, it's not human. Our journey is an unpredictable ride of ups and downs.

6/5/17

We love our roses. They remind us of our Penny girl. Her heavenly mass also happened to be on the Feast day of St. Therese of Lisieux, also known as "The Little Flower," who passed on September 30, 1897 at 24 years old from illness. It is said that when you pray to Saint Therese of Lisieux she sends roses as a sign to let you know your prayers have been heard. This can be the scent of a rose, a rose itself, someone named Rose, they are all heavenly messages to let us know we have been heard. I love to smell the roses that John planted in our garden, and then pray... pray so very hard.

6/28/17

> "You will embark," he said "on a fair sea, and at times
> there will be fair weather, but not always. You will meet
> storms and overcome them. You will take it in turns to
> steer your boat through fair weather and foul. Never
> lose courage. Safe harbor awaits you both in the end."
> Daphne Du Maurier

What foul weather we are experiencing. This 9-month storm is in full
of rage mode. The waves are steep and dark and ugly and they obliterate
everything upon landing. Time and time again. Day in and day out.
We are soaked in sadness and anger and grief. Sometimes one of us will
grab that wheel and steer the boat out before the next thunderous wave
hits, but more often than not both captains are down, still trying to
gather themselves from the last hit. What do we do? There is no other
soul aboard. This is a magical boat made for two. So special. It's made
of everlasting love and the union of two souls and two bodies. How
could anyone take it over? They don't know the beautiful mechanics of
it. They didn't lay every board to fit perfectly, and deliciously love every
curve and space. They didn't feel the intensity of its joy. Only the two
captains know. It is their boat to steer. The panic. The fear. The pain.
The torture. The deep missing. The deep longing. The deep ache. The
why us. The I can't do this. The I don't know how we are going to make
it through. The will we survive? The look at those other little children,
how lucky their parents are. The jolts back to the hospital memories.
The images of your angel baby lying with tubes out of her mouth and
nose, motionless. The images of her beautiful head wrapped in white.
The blood on her perfect fingernail. The kissing her for the last time.
The "you know exactly what I mean." The "you just need to focus on
the baby coming." The stay strong. The "glad to see you are doing better." The thoughts as we sip and smile and nod. The "Oh I'm doing
OK." The "No it's not my first." The try not to ugly cry. The "you just
need to be strong for your spouse." The I can't breathe. All we can do is
pray as we gasp for breath and life. We are not steering this boat, after
all. God is our captain.

8/1/17

John and I have talked about this a lot lately. It is a mentally exhausting job to CHOOSE joy in our days and to focus on love, the giving and receiving and reminding ourselves that Penny lived two and a half years of daily joy and love. What a weave of magic the three of us were, and still are. Yes, she did have some weeks of illness but even then she had us right by her side singing songs, playing with her beloved stickers and Play-Doh, holding her when she'd cry from needles, breastfed when she needed the comfort of her mama, danced with her when she needed the tender touch of her daddy.

8/9/17

God is the source of strength in which I trust. I am constantly reminding myself that my strength in healing lies not in my actions alone but first and foremost in the power of prayer. If you don't know how to pray, or what to say, or have never given God much thought, just say in the quiet of your heart, "Dear Lord, I am willing to see things differently, please help me." "Dear God, I am willing to see my pain differently." In offering up my pain to God, a spiritual alchemy is ignited and my thoughts become more restful. I am then more willing to accept things, people and situations as they are. As I put the pain in His hands, so the pain is altered. The power of God's grace is no magical fantasy, it is real Power, and the fact that I can move forward each day with an enormous hole in my heart, and still feel joyful moments most days, is a testament to the work of God's healing grace. We all look up, and there, is the face of God our Father. Tears of healing from Him drench every cell. Bow down with thanks and now, grow.

10/7/17

My two girls. One in my belly. One in my heart. I wish I could say I was on top of the moon with excitement for baby sister's arrival but it's more a wild tornado of deep Penny grief and excited anticipation that swirls inside daily. I cry one minute. I feel excited in the very next. I know this is OK. I know this is natural. But it doesn't make it any less confusing and overwhelming. Rewinding back to days before April 28th 2014, what a different chapter of our story we were on. Such innocence, such pure excitement, and the nervousness of a first time mama and daddy. Now we face the question of whether Penny's baby sister will be OK; will we be OK; will I be a neurotic hypochondriac mama; will we be able to enjoy our baby's magnificence without being pained by our Penny's baby memories? Furthermore, how will we always keep Penny alive in our daily lives while still experiencing the joy of her baby sister? How will we make sure of the presence of her sister's light even through our sadness? The list of questions goes on and on.

But, again and again, I remind myself that my strength lies not only in me, but even more so in my trust in God's protecting love and the healing power of the Holy Spirit in Christ. I hand it all over to Him. And when I feel fear again, a beautiful blond girl taps me on my heart and reminds me to hand it over again to Him, and I am free to just love.

* * *

If there is a message I would like to leave for others who are grieving, it is simply the following. When faced with loss and suffering of this magnitude (i.e., the loss of a child), grief is not a choice. It is inevitable. However, in the midst of grief, one can choose either to harden one's heart, concealing it from life's future blessings, joys, and gifts, or one can choose to keep one's heart malleable, opening it to life's future blessings, joys, and gifts. Yes, even amid great pain, one can choose joy; one can choose life. God's love is creative, and in the midst of grief, one is asked to trust that He will create again. There is no *plan* or *deadline* for grief; it is as unique as the person one grieves. Grief demands one's attention and so one devotes time to grieve—but to grieve in hope, trusting that the loving Lord is present and active, creating new life, while at the same time, honoring the memories.

Genevieve Deely
November 30, 2017

CONTENTS

Acknowledgements

As always, I am grateful to the administration, staff, and colleagues of Sacred Heart Major Seminary, Detroit, Michigan, who provide me with a sanctuary, indeed, a home for teaching and writing.

Thanks are also due to those individuals who gave me their comments on chapters of this book: Peter Williamson, Marsha Daigle Williamson, and Mary Healy. I am also grateful for the editorial assistance of Sr. Mary Boersen, SGL.

Chapters 2-4 of this present book are based on an essay that was produced in the context of a 1999 Summer Seminar in Christian Scholarship, Calvin College, Grand Rapids, Michigan. It was published in *Christian Faith and the Problem of Evil*, Editor, Peter van Inwagen (Grand Rapids, MI: Eerdmans, 2004), "The Gospel of Redemptive Suffering: Reflections on John Paul II's Salvifici Doloris" (111-147).

This book is chiefly dedicated to my beloved granddaughter, Penelope Grace Deely (2014-2016). But I thought it fitting to dedicate it as well to my daughter and son-in-law, Genevieve and John Deely, Penny's parents. They grieved but not without hope (1 Thess 4:13). Their trust in God's grace and love, which gave them hope, even in the midst of their grieving, was as an anchor for their soul, firm and secure (Heb 6:19). My abundant thanks to Genevieve for writing the Foreword.

I am also grateful to Eric and Linda Wolf of Lectio Publishing for their positive response to my proposal for writing a book that gave a response to the question of the Christian meaning of human suffering in light of the passing of Penelope. I am also grateful to them for including Genevieve's Foreword and the photos of Penny in this book.

I am indebted and thankful to St. John Paul II (1920-2005) for his writings, especially but not only those that play a key role in this book on the Christian understanding of human suffering. He continues to be an important stimulus to my own philosophical and theological work, my teaching, and, last but not least, the dynamics of an authentic Catholic understanding of true spirituality. "Those with insight shall shine brightly like the splendor of the firmament" (Dan 12:3).

> May God grant that I speak with judgment and have thoughts worthy of what I have received, for he is the guide even of wisdom and the corrector of the wise. For both we and our words are in his hand, with all our understanding, too. (Wis 7:15-16)

List of Abbreviations

C&CC	Joseph Ratzinger, *Christianity and the Crisis of Cultures*. Translated by Brian McNeil (San Francisco: Ignatius Press, 2006).
CCC	USCCB, *Catechism of the Catholic Church*.
CoC	John Paul II, *A Catechesis on the Creed*, vol. I, *God, Father, and Creator* (Boston: Pauline Books & Media, 1996). — vol. II, *Jesus, Son and Savior* (Boston: Pauline Books & Media, 1996).
DM	John Paul II, *Dives in Misericordia, Rich in Mercy*, Encyclical Letter, 30 November 1980.
FeR	John Paul II, *Fides et Ratio, On Faith and Reason*, Encyclical Letter, 14 September 1998.
GHJ	Jacques Maritain, *On the Grace and Humanity of Jesus*, trans. Joseph W. Evans (New York: Herder and Herder, 1969).
GS	Vatican Council II, *Gaudium et Spes: Pastoral Constitution on the Church in the Modern World*, 7 December 1965.
GWT	Francis A. Schaeffer, *The God Who is There* (Downers Grove, IL: Inter-Varsity Press, 1968).
HS	Berkouwer, G. C., *De Heilige Schrift* I-II (Kampen: J.H. Kok, 1966-1967). Translated and edited by Jack B. Rogers as *Holy Scripture* (Grand Rapids, MI: Eerdmans, 1975).
NGM	Pope Francis, *The Name of God is Mercy*, (New York: Random House, 2016).

MV	Pope Francis, *Misericordiae Vultus*, 11 April 2015.
OTD	Joseph Ratzinger, *Dogma and Preaching, Applying Christian Doctrine to Daily Life*, trans. Michael J. Miller and Matthew J. O'Connell, ed. Michael J. Miller (San Francisco: Ignatius Press, 2011), "On the Theology of Death," 243-54.
SD	John Paul II, *Salvifici Doloris, On the Christian Meaning of Human Suffering*, Apostolic Letter, 11 February 1984.
SI	Berkouwer, G. C., "Sacrificium Intellectus?," *Gereformeerd Theologisch Tijdschrift* 68 (August 1968).
VS	John Paul II, *Veritatis Splendor, The Splendor of Truth*, Encyclical Letter, 6 August 1993.

INTRODUCTION

Unanswered Prayers
and the Love of God

Perplexed, but not in despair. (2 Cor 4:8)

Suffering is an enigmatic fact which challenges every world view. It is especially difficult to see any meaning or purpose in the suffering, sometimes excruciating and awful, of small children. And when one personally suffers or those one loves do, one wants to know why. But even more, one wants some *way* of dealing with suffering which holds out hope, based not on illusion but on *truth*, that a new and better *life* awaits one after death.[1]

There is not a single aspect of the Christian message that is not in part an answer to the question of evil. (CCC §309)

*M*y heart is broken. My beloved granddaughter Penelope Grace Deely, only 2½ years old, died early Sunday morning, last September 25, at the Children's Hospital of Philadelphia. I was there with the family. In the end, her body proved defenseless against a virulent strain of meningitis. It had attacked her suddenly and swiftly. She was dead within thirty-six hours. As I write this book, my daughter Genevieve and her husband John are still trying, trusting in God, to make their way through their journey of pain and loss.[2]

Here follows an excerpt from the eulogy that Penelope's Grandmother, Marijke Lewis, gave before the funeral Mass on Saturday, October 1, 2016. It gives you a taste of who was beautiful Penelope.

When we've discussed the last few terrible days amongst

ourselves, what seems to come up so often is the most amazing way that everyone has pulled out all the stops to make what has been one's worst nightmare, turn into a time of a thousand moments of the most loving and heartfelt acts of human kindness. We are so very grateful and deeply moved by you all. Thank you. We are also amazed by the fact that so many people who have not even met Penny, say that in some way or the other, Penny has impacted their lives. We look around us now in this beautiful church and see so many of us here, friends and relatives from both families, co-workers, Penny's pre-school families, some Catholic, some Protestant or Jewish and friends with no formal faith at all. We are all joined here together under one roof to celebrate the life of one magnificent bright Light, Penny. How could it happen that a 3' blonde with magical eyes have so much impact to draw us all together in this way? Perhaps we can start by reflecting for a moment on her name and how Penny came to be called Penelope Grace: The choice of 'Penelope' was her parents' and it surprised us all. We had all consulted the Ultimate Book of All Knowledge and Wisdom—the Internet— and no one had come up with that name. But then we got to realize how well it suited the self-assured little girl with a vivacious and adorable personality. Bright and personable, very musical and funny. She possessed a vocabulary well beyond her age and even spoke in full sentences. Gen told me of a time when she was feeling a little down on one particular day. "Are you feeling sad, Mama?," she asked. "Would you like a hug?" Gen also told me of the times when they would be outside getting into the car or taking a walk and Penny would call out to neighbors with a bright hello and their name so crystal clear. She had been to school not even two weeks and loved it. She had made it to her first "no cry day" marker. She truly was the classic two-year-old going on sixty. That was the little girl we all got to know as "Penelope." The "Grace" part was my choice. I have always believed that it was a beautiful name but it also, significantly, points to the part of her name that will most apply to her and us from now on. I have always believed... that this name points to the fact that we cannot hope to go through the experiences that life throws at us without having a sense that God's Love and Grace are sustaining us through them all.

My youngest daughter Christine raised the question of unanswered prayer in connection with sweet Penny's death. Why would God not answer the prayers of so many people for Penny's life? Does unanswered prayer count against the love of God? That is the crucial question. "The silence of God is hardest to bear for those who believe that the God of our faith is the living God and not the 'gods' of whom the psalmist says: 'They have mouths but do not speak' (Ps 115:5)."[3] All things considered unanswered prayer does not count against the love of God for the fundamental reason that our lament has already been answered in the cross of Jesus Christ and through his Resurrection.

This is not the answer we want, unquestionably, but it is the only answer we have that puts our lamenting Penny's death in a right and hopeful perspective. "Through Christ and in Christ, the riddles of sorrow and death grow meaningful. Apart from His Gospel, they overwhelm us. Christ has risen, destroying death by His death" (GS §22).

Still, putting the question this way makes clear that for some people it isn't about whether God exists, or is sovereign in power and knowledge. Rather, it is about God's goodness, particularly his love.

As a committed Christian, in particular, a Catholic, how do I answer the spiritual perplexity—not despair!—occasioned by this question, not just for my daughter Christine, and others like her who have this vexing question, but for myself? Where's God? We walk by faith and not by sight, St. Paul tells us (2 Cor 5:7). He adds, we see through a glass darkly; we know in part (1 Cor 13:12). One implication of this limitation is that I do not know the answer to the question as to why the death of *this* child.

This child who was loved unconditionally and deeply. *This* child who responded unconditionally to her mother and father, Genevieve and John, with an equally deep love. *This* child, who was blond, with green/hazel tinted eyes, and to all who knew her was beautiful, amazing, a gift, and full of promise. *This* child, my Penelope, whose actual voice I will never hear again in this life. *This* child, who is unrepeatable, one of her kind, irreplaceable, leaves us with a hole in reality that will never be filled. How can I stand her absence? And why me? These are questions my daughter Genevieve has often expressed to me since sweet Penny's death.

Yes, we walk by faith and not by sight. Thus, given this limitation of what I can know, here and now, I am perplexed, but not troubled. My resolute belief in the goodness of a loving God, of the God of Abraham, Isaac, and Jacob, of the God and Father of our Lord Jesus Christ, is not shaken by the death of my beloved Penelope. I know who God is, and his revelation in the Holy Bible tells me several things that help me through my perplexity. Revelation has epistemic authority.

At root, then, what follows is a confession of faith regarding certain beliefs that I hold to be true, trusting in the epistemic authority of the Word of God. Whatever else I say and argue for in this book rests ultimately on the trustworthiness of God's Word as a source of knowledge. That is what it means to say that divine revelation has epistemic authority. Hence, the importance of Chapter 1 on biblical authority where I attempt to show the justification of affirming the Bible's epistemic authority as a reliable source of knowledge about God, man, and the world.

Furthermore, this book is a reflection on certain truths pertaining to the mystery of God and evil. To be clear, let me make the point that the Catholic sense of mystery is about truth, an excess, a superabundance, of wisdom and intelligibility.[4] "Mystery means never being able to say the last word about something which is rich in meaning; there is always more to say; there is not too little but too much to be known."[5]

In sum, let us not confuse mystery with contradiction, paradox, antinomy; otherwise, we may fall prey to the identification of mystery and irrationality.[6] These truths are such that they provide light in our path ahead. You see the truths of faith "are lights along the path of faith; they illuminate it and make it secure" (CCC §89). Affirming these revelational-based truths, as I unconditionally do, does not mean that I "have figured out what has perplexed so many people reflecting on the topic of God and evil."[7] As N.T. Wright says, "There is a noble Christian tradition which takes evil so seriously that it warns us against the temptation to 'solve' it in any obvious way. If you offer an analysis of evil which leaves us saying, 'Well, that's all right then, we now see how it happens and what to do about it,' you have belittled the problem."[8] And belittled the death of my beloved Penelope!

It is precisely in this connection that the distinction between problems and mystery is relevant. As John Paul II has stated: "In short, the knowledge proper to faith does not destroy the mystery; it only reveals it the more, showing how necessary it is for people's lives" (FeR §13). This distinction originates with the French Catholic philosopher Gabriel Marcel[9] and it is later developed by another French Catholic, the neo-Thomist philosopher Jacques Maritain.[10] The distinction highlights two different approaches that one can take in a field of inquiry, for instance, to issues of faith and theology. Maritain says, "It is a mystery and at the same time a problem, a mystery in regard to the thing, the object as it exists outside the mind, a problem in regard to our formulae."[11] For instance, that God is sovereign in goodness, knowledge, and power, on the one hand, and evil exists, evil suffered and done, on the other, is a mystery. Now, the way in which this mystery has been grasped and formulated is a problem. It is the former in the sense—keeping with our understanding of mystery above—that "no matter how much one said and no matter how true it may be, there is always more to be understood and articulated."[12]

In general, then, the theological enterprise, engaged in faith seeking understanding, is situated between mystery and problem. Thomas Weinandy correctly says, "The true goal of theological inquiry is not the resolution of theological *problems*, but the discernment of what the *mystery* of faith is. Because God, who can never be fully comprehended, lies at the heart of all theological inquiry, theology by its nature is not a problem-solving enterprise, but rather a mystery-discerning enterprise. . . . True Christian theology has to do with clarifying, and so developing, the understanding of the mysteries of faith and not the dissolving of the mysteries into complete comprehension."[13]

As the third epigraph to this chapter states, "*There is not a single aspect of the Christian message that is not in part an answer to the question of evil*" (CCC §309). Accordingly, there are several truths I will now highlight. The first truth I know is that death is an enemy in the Christian scheme of things, indeed, it is the last enemy to be destroyed (1 Cor

15:26); it is swallowed up in Christ's victory (1 Cor 15:54f.). Furthermore, in Penelope's death—in any child's death—I see the enemy of God. Moreover, Jesus himself assures us that "little children" belong to the Kingdom of God. "Let the little children come to me, and do not hinder them, for the kingdom of heaven belongs to such as these" (Matt 19:14; Mk 10:14; Lk 18:16). So, I think we can say here without any doubt that the suffering of children is contrary to the will of God and the law of his kingdom in Christ.[14]

In that light, I have the consolation that Penny is at peace because she was a baptized innocent and hence is in the presence of the Lord, seeing the face of God. What also brings consolation is the well-grounded hope that by God's merciful grace when I stand before him I will hear him say to me (adapting Luc Ferry[15]), "Come quickly, your granddaughter Penelope eagerly awaits you."

The second truth I know is—and it follows closely from the first— that I cannot find in the death of little children, in the death of *this* child, Penelope, an ultimate meaning or purpose, as if to say that Penny died for this or that reason. Yes, God can bring good out of the evils that he permits to exist by counteracting those evils with "ever novel opportunities for converting evil into goodness."[16] But what I cannot say, indeed, refuse to say, is that God directly intended Penny's death in order to bring about the good of "soul-making," in other words, giving one the opportunity to become a better person. Yes, Penny's parents, Genevieve and John, have grown in their faith in view of Penny's death, and we can see their increase in faith as a good side effect. But, in my view, what cannot be the case is that this "soul-making" is the reason for her death.

Still, as I will show in Chapter 3, in a general sense I hold with the Christian tradition that God's goodness and providence is defensible in the face of evil and suffering. There are certain experiential cues, what Peter Berger calls signals of transcendence, that can be developed into philosophical arguments for God's existence. Briefly, one such cue is found in the very knowability or intelligibility of the world that drives our minds toward an affirmation of God's existence. That is:

> For some reason, the world has a structure such that
> human mind can penetrate it by means of its own pro-
> cesses of thought. How can we account for this fact? It

might have been the case that human beings had intelligence but that the world was not amenable to exploration by that intelligence. There could have been a lack of fit between the world and the human mind. But in point of fact, there is not; on the contrary, there is considerable harmony between them as, among other things, the fruits of scientific knowledge and technology demonstrate. It is argued, therefore, that the world's intelligibility requires us to posit the existence of a creative mind, analogous to but infinitely transcending the human mind, by which the cosmos was brought into being.[17]

Similarly, there is a theodicy (Greek: *theos*: God; *dikē*: justice) that helps us to make some rational sense of matters such as evil and suffering by explaining the justice of God in the face of the counterevidence of evil and suffering. Still, the Christian tradition has long recognized that there are unfathomable depths to evil that are only answered by Christ's cross and resurrection. In short, radical evil is rationally inscrutable, in particular, evils such as the death of my beloved Penelope.

Please don't misunderstand me. I don't believe that death and evil have the last word, as if life is meaningless, a matter of blind fate, or wild chance. "God is master of the world and of its history. . . . With infinite wisdom and goodness God freely willed to create a world 'in a state of journeying' toward its ultimate perfection" (CCC §§310, 314). The Gospel brings us the good news that God's will cannot ultimately be defeated. Indeed, it assures me—and I trust in this truth with everything that is in me—that victory over evil and death—and hence victory over Penelope's death—has already been accomplished by Christ through his cross and resurrection (1 Cor 15:54-55).

In Chapter 2, then, I will argue that the problem of evil and suffering cannot be grappled with merely in terms of the theodicies within the arguments of philosophical theology (CCC §§31-34), such as, the free-will defense, although these arguments definitely have their place. For we cannot abdicate the use of reason, leaving the question of God, evil, and suffering entirely to faith. "The presence of evil must be *shown* not to exclude the idea of a good Creator. . . . The philosopher rightly insists that the idea of an omnipotent, good God be shown to be compatible with the actual existence of evil. Reason modestly yet legitimately demands only to perceive how an open conflict between a good God and an evil world is *not inevitable*."[18]

Still, as N.T. Wright correctly says, we must see "the cross as part of both the analysis and the solution of that problem."[19] In general, as John Paul II wrote, "The philosopher who learns humility will also find courage to tackle questions that are difficult to resolve if the data of revelation are ignored—for example, the problem of evil and suffering, the personal nature of God and the question of the meaning of life or, more directly, the radical metaphysical question, 'Why is there something rather than nothing'?" (FeR §76). In short, "Revealed truth offers the fullness of light and will therefore illumine the path of philosophical inquiry" (FeR §79). In this chapter, I will provide a justification for Christian beliefs to act as control beliefs for the devising and weighing of a philosophical account of the problem of God, evil, and suffering.

The third truth I know is that there is a battle of good and evil—and death is evil, an enemy of God!— darkness and light, truth and falsehood, life and death raging all around us. But as Christians we live in anticipation of the day when God will make all things new. This promise includes the dwelling of God with his people, with "God wiping away all tears from their eyes; and there shall be no more death, neither sorrow, nor crying, neither shall there be any more pain" (Rev 21:3-5).

For now, we must pick up our cross and follow Christ (Matt 16:24) to his death on the cross and his resurrection, uniting our sufferings with his sufferings. We are learning how to suffer. We know that life not death has the last word. We have the promise that his grace is sufficient to help us carry the burden of this cross of my beloved Penny's death (2 Cor 12:9). Therefore, in Chapter 4, I will explain John Paul II's notion of redemptive suffering.

Finally, I have been listening a lot recently to the Australian Evangelical Christian group Hillsong United in the context of Psalm 69. As N.T. Wright remarks, "The psalmist describes his despair in terms of being up to his neck in deep water." Yet, adds Wright, "this is held within a context where YHWH [the biblical name of the God of Israel] is already known as the one who rules the raging of the sea and even makes it praise him (Ps 69:1, 34)."[20] As we read later in Psalm 93, "Mightier than the thunder of the great waters, mightier than the breakers of the sea—the Lord on high is mighty"(v. 4). Perhaps I was being prepared for this lamentation over Penny's death because I have been particularly impressed by Hillsong United's song, "Oceans (Where Feet May Fail)." Indeed, I have adopted one of their verses as this book's title.

Here, too, there is an emphasis, not only on the sufficiency of God's grace, but also, as Penny's mother Genevieve wrote, on God's trustworthiness in steering us through the turbulent waters. "All we can do is pray as we gasp for breath and life. We are not steering this boat, after all." This is right. We read in the New Testament gospel, Matt 14:27, when the apostles are fearful of the waves: "But immediately Jesus spoke to them, saying, "Take heart, it is I; do not be afraid." It is his grace that has helped all of us, particularly Penny's parents, Genevieve and John, to deal with their pain and loss. In keeping with the image of water rising as waves, I will end this Introduction with a taste of Hillsong United's song:

> You call me out upon the waters
> The great unknown where feet may fail
> And there I find You in the mystery
> In oceans deep
> My faith will stand
>
> And I will call upon Your name
> And keep my eyes above the waves
> When oceans rise
> My soul will rest in Your embrace
> For I am Yours and You are mine
>
> Your grace abounds in deepest waters
> Your sovereign hand
> Will be my guide
> Where feet may fail and fear surrounds me
> You've never failed and You won't start now
> So I will call upon Your name.

Notes

1. Germain Grisez, *The Way of the Lord Jesus*, vol. 2, 31.
2. See the Foreword to this book where my daughter, Genevieve Deely, gives her account of this journey.

3. Gustavo Gutiérrez, *On Job*, xv.

4. Ibid., xl: "[I]it is important to keep in mind from the very outset that theological thought about God is *thought about a mystery*. . . . Let me make it clear, however, that when we talk of 'mystery' with the Bible in mind, we do not mean something that is hidden and must *remain hidden*. The 'mystery' in this case must rather be expressed, not concealed; communicated, not kept to itself. E. Jüngel puts it well: 'the fact of having to be revealed belongs to the essence of mystery'."

5. John Saward, "Christ The Light of the Nations, Part II." Paul Helm agrees: "We may be able to clarify the mystery further, but a Christian theologian is certainly not in the business of eliminating divine mysteries as a matter of principle" (*Faith, Form, and Fashion*, 32).

6. Sproul, *Chosen by God*, 43-47, has a brief but helpful discussion of the differences between mystery, on the one hand, and contradiction, paradox, and antinomy, on the other. See also, Roger E. Olson, "A Crucial but Much Ignored (or Misunderstood) Distinction for Theology: "Mystery" versus "Contradiction."

7. Brian Davies, O.P., *Thomas Aquinas on God and Evil*, 129.

8. N. T. Wright, *Evil and the Justice of God*, 20.

9. Gabriel Marcel, *The Mystery of Being*, I, 204-19.

10. Jacques Maritain, *A Preface to Metaphysics*, 3-11.

11. Ibid., 4.

12. Weinandy, *Does God Suffer?*, 31.

13. Ibid., 32, 35.

14. Hart, *The Doors of the Sea, Where was God in the Tsunami?*, 34.

15. Ferry, *A Brief History of Thought*, 263.

16. Dupre, "Philosophy and the Mystery of Evil," 58.

17. Nichols, *The Shape of Catholic Theology*, 56-59, and at 59. See also, Lonergan, *Method in Theology*, 101-103. Lonergan argues that the question of God arises in respect of the presupposition that the universe in intelligible. "Once that is granted, there arises the question whether the universe could be intelligible without having an intelligent ground. But that is the question about God." Furthermore, "The facts of good and evil, of progress and decline, raise questions about the character of our universe. . . . We praise progress and denounce every manifestation of decline. But is the universe on our side, or are we just gamblers and, if we are gamblers, are we not perhaps fools, individually struggling for authenticity and collectively endeavoring to snatch progress from the ever mounting welter of decline. . . . Does there or does there not necessarily exist a transcendent, intelligent ground of the universe? Is that ground or are we the primary instance of moral consciousness? Are cosmogenesis, biological evolution, historical process basically cognate to us as moral beings or are they indifferent and so alien to us. Such is the question of God."

18. Dupre, "Philosophy and the Mystery of Evil," 54.

19. Wright, *Evil and the Justice of God*, 77.

20. Ibid., 14.

CHAPTER 1

Biblical Authority?

To be sure, in Christianity there is a primacy of the *logos*, of the word, over silence; God *has* spoken. God is word. . . . The comfortable attempt to spare oneself the belief in the mystery of God's mighty actions in this world and yet at the same time to have the satisfaction of remaining on the foundation of the biblical message leads nowhere; it measures up neither to the honesty of reason nor to the claims of faith. One cannot have both the Christian faith and "religion within the bounds of pure reason"; a choice is unavoidable. He who believes will see more and more clearly, it is true, how rational it is to have faith in the love that has conquered death.[1]

In order that men might have knowledge of God, free of doubt and uncertainty, it was necessary for Divine matters to be delivered to them by way of faith, being told of them, as it were, by God Himself who cannot lie.[2]

And we also thank God constantly for this, that when you received the word of God, which you heard from us, you accepted it not as the word of men but as what it really is, the word of God, which is at work in you believers. (1 Thess 2:13)

What makes human life meaningful, even in the face of death and decay[?] This vexing question occupies the attention of the late Paul Kalanithi, a neurosurgeon who died in March 2015. Although Kalanithi was a man of science who studied biology and neuroscience, he never really accepted the idea that science could explain everything.* He did consider the possibility of a material conception of reality, namely, that matter is ultimately all there is, that immaterial realities, such as souls and God are outmoded concepts, that man is simply the chance product of matter in motion (see 170-171). But eventually he came to see that "to make science the arbiter of metaphysics [of what is ultimately real] is to banish not only God from the world but also love, hate, meaning—to consider a world that is self-evidently *not* the world we live in" (169).

Yes, man is a biological organism subject to the laws of physics and chemistry. Yet, he is at the same desperately searching for meaning, that is, "for human connection." Kalanithi struggled with the challenge of facing death and the knowledge that he is surely dying in this light.

What makes human life worth living in this context? "Meaning, while a slippery concept, seemed inextricable from human relationships and moral values" (31). It is "relationships that give life meaning" (34). In his search to understand the human condition, then, Kalanithi sought a "deeper understanding of a life of the mind." He adds, "I studied literature and philosophy to understand what makes life meaningful, studied neuroscience and worked in an fMRI lab to understand how the brain could give rise to an organism capable of finding meaning in the world, and enriched my relationships with a circle of dear friends" (35).

Furthermore, in the search for meaning, many people turn to God. But according to Kalanithi, God and meaning don't necessarily go together. In other words, believing in meaning doesn't necessarily mean that you must also believe in God. Besides, "science provides no basis for God." In short, since "all knowledge is scientific knowledge" (169), this claim raises the question whether belief in God is rational. Not according to Kalanithi. "There is no proof of God; therefore, it is unreasonable to *believe* in God" (168).

How does Kalanithi know that there are no such arguments? It isn't that he examines the arguments for God's existence and finds them wanting. Not at all. He simply *assumes* that to be the case. They seem to him to be passé, no longer needing refutation. On this matter, he

* Paul Kalanithi, *When Breath Becomes Air*, 42, 30. In this section, page references to this work appear in parentheses within the text.

couldn't be more mistaken given the revival of interest among contemporary philosophers in arguments for the existence of God.[3] I'll consider some of these arguments, particularly as they pertain to the matter of God and evil, later in this book.

For now, I want to note that, significantly, Kalanithi also identifies knowing God by way of proof or argument with knowing anything at all about God. This means that rationality, according to him, is reduced not only to scientific knowledge, but also that it is the only way to know God. But this identifies arguments as the only source of knowledge of God, suggesting that such arguments are necessary in holding Christian beliefs rationally. I think that this identification is mistaken: arguments for God's existence are available, but not necessary for being rational in holding Christian beliefs to be true.

We don't yet have the full picture of Kalanithi's view. Although he claims that there are no proofs of God's existence, that doesn't mean, according to him, that we shouldn't reflect on "the most central aspects of human life: hope, fear, love, hate, beauty, envy, honor, weakness, striving, suffering, virtue" (170). Yes, there is a fundamental gap between these central aspects and scientific rationality. But the basic reality of human life stands compellingly against a material conception of reality, against the idea that man is just the chance product of matter in motion. So, in this light, Kalanithi "returned to the central values of Christianity—sacrifice, redemption, forgiveness—because I found them so compelling" (171).

Still, Kalanithi adds, he couldn't say anything definitive about God. Indeed, he holds that it is impossible to credit "revelation with any epistemic authority." In other words, divine revelation—in short, the Scriptures—are not a trustworthy source of knowledge and hence one would not be rational in holding its claims to be true. Says Kalanithi, "We are all reasonable people—revelation is not good enough. Even if God spoke to us, we'd discount it as delusional" (172). Delusional? Then in what sense, if any, are the central values of Christianity compelling?

Kalanithi has no answer to this question. Indeed, as far as I can see, given that he contrasts faith/revelation and rationality, that means, in effect, as I understand Kalanithi, that the Bible is not a trustworthy source of knowledge, in particular, the New Testament, and hence believing its claims about sacrifice, redemption, forgiveness, all rooted in the redeeming acts of God in Christ, the Incarnate Word of God, assumes that faith is distinguished from rationality by virtue of having beliefs that are rationally unjustified. It is precisely this claim that I will contest in the remainder of this chapter. The Bible does have epistemic authority and it is reasonable to believe that it does.

Can Agnosticism be a Solution?

Agnosticism is one of the most common responses to the type of position that Kalanithi takes. The Bible's lack epistemic authority and hence Christian beliefs are unjustified. The root meaning of "agnostic" is from Ancient Greek: *a-*, meaning "without," and *gnōsis,* meaning "knowledge." In short, then, according to the philosopher William L. Rowe: "agnosticism is the view that human reason is incapable of providing sufficient rational grounds to justify either the belief that God exists or the belief that God does not exist."[4] The only recourse the agnostic offers us is to suspend judgment regarding Christian beliefs in view of the alleged insufficiency of evidence. But it is precisely this agnostic stance of the faith-vetoer's position that I will challenge, with a big help from my friend and philosopher, William James (1842-1910), before going on to lay out a positive case for the justification of Christian belief.[5]

Understanding some preliminaries is important to James's critique of agnosticism as the only reasonable response to the alleged insufficiency of evidence. First, as would-be knowers we have the epistemic responsibility to know the truth and to avoid error. Second, which one of these aspects of our responsibility as would-be knowers has priority depends on our belief policy. For instance, if we hold that we ought to suspend judgment because of alleged insufficient evidence, then, one will prioritize the relationship between these two duties by regarding the "avoidance of error as more imperative, and let truth take its chance." Vice versa, others, such as James, have regarded the "chase for truth as paramount, and the avoidance of error as secondary" (WB, 18). It is the former position that James identifies as the agnostic stance urging us to the agnostic choice to suspend judgment as the only reasonable one: "*Better risk loss of truth than chance of error*"—that is your faith-vetoer's exact position" (WB, 26).

Third, the choices we make are driven by not only our intellect but also our will, indeed, our whole nature, what James calls our passional nature. This means the agnostic is also making a choice, not merely on intellectual grounds, but also particularly in light of the just-mentioned belief policy when he urges us to suspend judgment. James opposes this choice and its attendant belief policy with his own counter policy:

> The thesis I defend is, briefly stated, this: Our passional nature not only lawfully may, but must, decide an option between propositions, whenever it is a genuine option that cannot by its nature be decided on intellectual grounds; for to say, under such circumstances, "Do not decide, but leave the question open," is itself a passional decision—just like deciding yes or no—and is attended with same risk of losing the truth (WB, 11).

Four, James's counter policy raises the question regarding the conditions under which I am justified in risking that the beliefs I hold are true. There are certain elements in the epistemic situation of a would-be knower facing insufficient evidence. Under what conditions would he be justified in holding certain beliefs to be true, in taking an epistemic risk that they are true? The beliefs in question must involve a *living* option, a *momentous* option, and a *forced* option. A brief explanation of each of what each these qualifications mean is required before going forward.

Consider the option that is foundational to this book's approach to the question of God, evil, suffering, and death. James identifies two affirmations that are characteristic of religion, and, I would add, particularly of Christianity. In my own words, the first affirmation holds to be true the proposition that God is sovereign in goodness, knowledge, and power and hence he has the last word over evil, suffering, and death. In short, life not death is the final word in view of the passion, death, and resurrection of Jesus Christ. The second affirmation is, says James, "[W]e are better off even now if we believe the first affirmation to be true" (WB, 26). This option, then, with its two-fold affirmation is a *living* possibility for one who is considering whether it is rational to hold it to be true. It is a *momentous* option if "we are supposed to gain, even now, by our belief, and to lose by our non-belief, a certain vital good" (WB, 26). My thesis is this: knowing that our lament has already been answered in the cross of Jesus Christ and through his resurrection is a vital good that puts the death of my beloved granddaughter, Penelope, in a right and hopeful perspective. "Through Christ and in Christ, the riddles of sorrow and death grow meaningful. Apart from His Gospel, they overwhelm us. Christ has risen, destroying death by His death" (GS §22).

In addition, this option is a *forced* one if you can't really sit on the fence, so to speak, such that you must choose in practice between two alternatives. Joseph Ratzinger clearly states the alternatives: "either to live as if God did not exist or else to live as if God did exist and was the decisive reality of my existence" (C&CC, 88). But someone may respond to James's insistence that we are compelled to choose one or the other alternative by urging us to avoid either option, to remain agnostic, and hence suspend judgment. But does agnosticism really mean that we avoid taking an option? Or is it rather that we have opted for a particular kind of risk? The risk James has in mind is driven by the belief I mentioned earlier: "Better risk loss of truth than chance of error." In this light, James's answer is crystal clear:

> We cannot escape the issue by remaining sceptical and waiting for more light, because, although we do avoid error in that way if religion be untrue, we lose the good, if it be true, just as certainly as if we positively chose to disbelieve. It is as if a man should hesitate indefinitely to ask a certain woman to marry him because he was not perfectly sure that she would prove an angel after he brought her home. Would he not cut himself off from that particular angel-possibility as decisively as if he went and married someone else? (WB, 26)

In other words, the faith-vetoer's choice does not at all avoid in practice taking a position. In practice, adds James, "he is actively playing his stake as much as the believer is; he is backing the field against the religious hypothesis, just as the believer is backing the religious hypothesis against the field."[6] Essentially, then, James is suggesting that this belief policy drives our agnostic choice because it is suggested that when considering a religious proposition yielding to our fear of being erroneous about the truth of this proposition "is wiser and better than to yield to our hope that it may be true" (WB, 27). James advances the argument at this point by arguing that since agnostic choice is driven by one or another belief policy—either the one that regards the search for truth as primary, and the avoidance of error as secondary, or vice-versa—then it isn't that the agnostic's choice, the faith-vetoer's position, is driven by the force of reason alone whereas the believer's choice is driven by faith alone. Rather, these choices are driven by different belief-policies, and which belief-policy is more warranted than the other? In other words, why does the belief-policy driving the agnostic's choice "demonstrate superior rationality to the contrary option?"[7] James replies:

> I, for one, can see no proof; and I simply refuse obe-
> dience to the scientist's command to imitate his kind
> of option, in a case where my own stake is important
> enough to give me the right to choose my own form of
> risk. If religion be true and the evidence for it be still
> insufficient, I do not wish, by putting your extinguisher
> upon my nature (which feels to me as if it had after all
> some business in this matter), to forfeit my sole chance
> in life of getting upon the winning side—that chance
> depending, of course, on my willingness to run the risk
> of acting as if my passional need of taking the world
> religiously might be prophetic and right (WB, 27).

James, then, concludes:

> I, therefore, cannot see my way to accepting the ag-
> nostic rules for truth-seeking, or willfully agree to keep
> my willing nature out of the game. I cannot do so for
> the plain reason, that *a rule of thinking which would
> absolutely prevent me from acknowledging certain kinds of
> truth if those kinds of truth were really there, would be an
> irrational rule.* That for me is the long and short of the
> formal logic of the situation, no matter what the kinds
> of truth might materially be (WB, 28-29).

There are two possible ways to understand James's argument; one, a weaker reading; and two, a stronger reading. On the one hand, there is the weaker reading of it such that James, is refuting the idea that reason compels one to the agnostic choice. In other words, there is no case to be made for the "supposed superior rationality of the 'agnostic veto' on belief—don't believe in God until you have overwhelming evidence."

Consequently, James is simply arguing that there is "an option between two risks of loss of truth," as Taylor puts it, and one, he adds, "should be free to choose his own kind of risk."[8] Better risk loss of truth than chance of error; or vice-versa, risk chance of error than loss of truth. On the weaker reading, I am within my epistemic rights to take the risk to believe that the religious beliefs I hold are true. Says James, "We have the [epistemic] right to believe at our own risk any hypothesis that is live enough to tempt our will" (WB, 29). On the other hand, there is the stronger reading of James's argument where the agnostic stance is the less rational choice than the believer's choice. On the weaker reading our choice leads us to embrace something of vital significance, a vital good, momentously significant, that would otherwise remain closed to us without risking the choice of holding it to be true. Hence, that choice is the more rational one, according to James.

> *In concreto*, the freedom to believe can only cover living options which the intellect of the individual cannot by itself resolve; and living options never seem absurdities to him who has them to consider. When I look at the religious question as it really puts itself to concrete men, and when I think of all the possibilities which both practically and theoretically it involves, then this command that we shall put a stopper on our heart, instincts, and courage, and *wait*—acting of course meanwhile more or less as if religion were *not* true—till doomsday, or till such time as our intellect and senses working together may have raked in evidence enough—this command, I say, seems to me the queerest idol ever manufactures in the philosophic cave.... Indeed, we *may* wait if we will—I hope you do not think that I am denying that—but if we do so, we do so at our peril as much as if we believed. In either case we *act*, taking our life in our hands (WB, 29-30).

In light of James's argument, let's look back briefly to Kalanithi's position that the Bible's lack epistemic authority, there are no arguments supporting Christian beliefs, and hence they are unjustified. Agnosticism is one of the most common responses to this type of position. Kalanithi did not appear to take an agnostic stance since he says that he found compelling the central values of Christianity—sacrifice, redemption, forgiveness. Still, he doesn't tell us why he finds them compelling and how he is justified in embracing them. Given his belief policy that Christian beliefs are unjustifiable, we can understand why some have concluded that suspension of judgment, the agnostic's choice, is the only reasonable choice.

What have we gained from James's argument refuting the agnostic's stance as the most reasonable choice? Briefly, we are free to exercise the responsible choice of choosing the risk of believing that the beliefs we hold are true even though we might be in error. This freedom is reasonable because the agnostic's choice is not driven by a superior rationality that compels us to suspend judgment. Suspending judgment involves the act of forgoing the risk of embracing new truth just as surely as judging negatively that there is no truth there to know. Hence, the religious option is a forced one. Furthermore, on a strong reading of James's argument the more reasonable choice, and hence the preferable one, given that the religious option is live, momentous, and forced, is "to run the risk of acting as if my passional need of taking the world religiously might be prophetic and right." In sum, "All this is on the supposition that it really may be prophetic and right, and that, even to us who are discussing the matter, religion is a live hypothesis which may be true" (WB, 27). Acting on that supposition puts us in a better position to affirm that our lament has already been answered in the cross of Jesus Christ and through his resurrection. This affirmation is a vital good that puts the death of my beloved granddaughter, Penelope, in a right and hopeful perspective.

Yet, I think there is a more positive case to be made for being justified in holding Christian beliefs to be true. I now turn to making that case by appealing to testimony.

Testimony

I will now show that appeals to testimony may provide a justification for belief such that no additional reason, that is, nontestimonial arguments, is required to justify belief. I call this approach "modest testimonial foundationalism" à la the Christian epistemology of Protestant philosopher Alvin Plantinga.[9] This is a form of "weak" foundationalism, but a foundationalism nonetheless because "it is rational to accept certain propositions without basing that acceptance on any other beliefs or propositions."[10] On this view, says Wahlberg, "testimony could be regarded as an *irreducible*, or sui generis, source of epistemic justification, in the same way that perception, inference, and memory are. If *anti-reductionism* with respect to testimonial knowledge is correct, then a satisfactory justification for believing that *p* can be that one has been told that *p*."[11]

In this connection, I now turn to consider the claim that divine revelation may be understood as a species of testimony. Its testimonial authority is such that it is both the independent ground of assent, epistemologically speaking, as well as the means of faith's knowledge of God, giving us testimonial knowledge.[12]

I consider here the doxastic practice of faith. A doxastic practice is a way of forming beliefs and epistemically evaluating them. Such practices include perception, memory, reasoning (demonstrative or inductive), and human testimony. I will now flesh out a little bit how the practice of human testimony involves an acceptance of statements that something is the case; in other words, "believing that" something is the case because what is believed must be something that is objectively true or false. In John Henry Newman's sermon, "Religious Faith Rational," he describes faith as "*reliance on the words of another.*"[13] As Elizabeth Anscombe puts it: testimony involves "believing *x* that *p*."[14] Newman's aim is to defend "faith as trust in another" as rationally justified and hence yielding testimonial knowledge; but he also puts the emphasis on "faith is no irrational or strange principle of conduct in the concerns of this life."[15] Indeed, there are many things that we would not know without trusting others.

The importance of testimony subordinates seeing to hearing[16] in the acquisition of justified true belief about a whole range of matters; scientific, historical, moral, theological, and many others.[17] In John Paul II's own words, "there are in the life of a human being many more truths which are simply believed than truths which are acquired by way of personal verification" (FeR §31). We still need to ask, "What, then, convinces us of it? The *report of others*? —this trust, this faith in testimony which, when religion is concerned, then, and only then, the proud and sinful would fain call irrational."[18] Newman replies, "We act upon our trust in them implicitly, because common sense tells us, that with proper caution and discretion, faith in others is perfectly safe and rational."[19] But what is it about the *report of others* that makes it rational to accept the word of another? Why is it rational to trust testimony?

In light of this question, I am now ready to ask what, then, is testimony? And why is it reasonable for one to accept the word of another, in short, testimony, as a source of epistemic justification such that no additional reason is required to justify belief?[20]

Helpful in this connection is, however, Kevin Vanhoozer's succinct definition of testimony, which holds also for our convictions grounded in divine testimony. Enlisting his definition, we can say that testimony is "a speech act in which the witness's very act of stating p is offered as evidence 'that p', it being assumed that the witness has the relevant competence or credentials to state truly 'that p'."[21] The testimony of such persons has "assertoric authority," meaning thereby "telling someone *that something is the case*."[22] On this account of testimony, Garcia rightly states, we accept the truth of statements that such-and-such is the case, the truth of statements that we do not see directly for ourselves but which it is reasonable to accept on the trustworthy word of others who are "in a *privileged position to know it*."[23]

Therefore, one may suggest the following justification for the epistemic authority of testimony, namely, accepting something because of who says it such that this person has assertoric authority. According to Linda Zagzebski:

> The epistemic authority of another person is justified for me by my conscientious judgment that I am more likely to form a true belief and avoid a false belief if I believe what the authority tells me than if I try to figure out what to believe myself.[24]

Newman suggests this notion of assertoric authority as well when he writes, "We constantly believe things even against our own judgment; i.e. when we think our informant likely to know more about the matter under consideration than ourselves, which is the precise case in the question of religious faith. And thus from reliance on others we acquire knowledge of all kinds and proceed to reason, judge, decide, act, form plans for the future."[25] Appeals to testimonial authority, then, can provide a reason for belief, and hence as such believing testimony is rational. Alvin Plantinga helps us to understand why it is rational to trust in others: "A belief is rational if it is produced by cognitive faculties that are functioning properly and successfully aimed at truth (i.e., aimed at the production of true beliefs)."[26]

All this may well be true regarding the testimonial knowledge that is the ordinary stuff of human life. But the knowledge of divine revelation passes beyond the boundaries of that knowledge. Ratzinger describes the problem here:

> Consequently, in this field there is no one in whom we could put our trust or to whose specialist knowledge we could refer, since no one could have a direct knowledge of such realities on the basis of his own personal studies. This means that we are confronted once again, and in an even more urgent fashion, with the problem: Is this type of faith compatible with modern critical knowledge? (C&CC, 84)

Are we, then, back to the dead-end of Kalanithi's denial of the Bible's epistemic authority and hence the unjustified nature of those who believe his claims? What exactly appears to be missing? In the doxastic practice of faith, says John Paul:

> "To believe" means to accept and to acknowledge as true and corresponding to reality the content of what is said, that is, the content of the words of another person . . . by reason of his credibility. This credibility determines in a given case the particular authority of the person—the authority of truth. So then by saying "I believe," we express at the same time a double reference: to the person and to the truth; to the truth in consideration of the person who *enjoys special claims* to credulity (FeR §31).

Credibility, then, is "*the property of a testimony.*"[27] For it is the person to whose testimony the assent is given in view of his special claim to credibility, resulting from his possession of the relevant credentials or competence to state truly the truth of the statement that something is the case.

'Believing' then involves not only believing that something is true but also believing in a person, the latter act characteristically being thought of as a matter of trust. And it is precisely this character of faith involving an appeal to what another has *seen* for himself, and which consequently grounds his credibility, that is the decisive element "lacking in supernatural-religious faith," or so it appears, says Ratzinger. He explains:

> This seemed to be the core of the problem of religious faith; but now we must say that impression was misleading. In supernatural faith, too, there are a multitude who live from a small number of persons: and this small number lives for the multitude. Similarly, in the things of God we are not *all* like blind people who grope their way forward in the dark. Here, too, there are persons who are permitted *to see*: Christ says of the father of the great family of Israel, "Abraham. . . *saw* [my day] and was glad" (John 8:56). Christ is there, at the very center of history, as the great man who sees, and all his words flow from his immediate contact with the Father. As for us, the word that refers to our situation is: "He who has seen *me* has seen the Father" (John 14:9). In its innermost essence, the Christian faith is a participation in this act whereby Jesus *sees*. His act of seeing makes possible his word, which is the authentic expression of what he sees. Accordingly, what Jesus sees is the point of reference for our faith, the specific place where it is anchored (C&CC, 105).

In short, Ratzinger is arguing that the justification of our trust in the Bible's testimonial knowledge of what Jesus Christ and the saints *see* is the reference point of our Christian beliefs, and, consequently, the guarantee of our being justified in holding these beliefs to be true. Hence, the decisive element is not lacking in supernatural-religious faith.

But this justification is not merely an intellectual act. Faith, which includes believing, says John Paul II, "involves an interpersonal relationship and brings into play not only a person's capacity to know [the truth] but also the deeper capacity to entrust oneself to others, to enter into a relationship with them which is intimate and enduring" (FeR §13). Thus, "to believe in," "to have faith in," "to entrust yourself to," comes to mean, in the pope's view, particularly in the case of divine faith, not simply a knowledge of propositional truths, but also a personal commitment to God, both a propositional knowledge and an affective trust, indeed, an act of the whole man. As John Paul II says, "In knowing by faith, man accepts the whole supernatural and salvific content of revelation as true. But at the same time, this fact introduces him into a profound personal relationship with God who reveals Himself" (FeR §44). Thus, through believing man participates in the knowledge of God himself because "in this case only, the primary person whose (inspired) testimony we believe is divine," and also, "the Spirit uses testimony to produce certain knowledge."[28] "Now faith is the assurance of things hoped for, the conviction of things not seen" (Heb 11:1).

This claim that believing man participates in God's knowledge of himself brings us back to the idea of the personalist character of faith for John Paul II, a view that Aquinas himself held. Briefly, "by saying 'I believe', we express at the same time a double reference: to the person and to the truth; to the truth in consideration of the person who *enjoys special claims* to credulity" (FeR §31). Therefore, faith does not involve merely believing a proposition, i.e., believing that *p* is true, but rather believing a person that what he says about *p* is true. Faith necessarily involves both a propositional attitude and an attitude toward a person.

This, too, is Aquinas's view: "Whoever believes, assents to someone's words; hence in every form of belief, the person to whose words assent is given seems to hold the principal place and to be the end, as it were, while the things by holding which one assents to that person hold a secondary place."[29] Hence, for Aquinas, "it belongs to faith to believe something and in someone."[30] At one and the same time, then, since God is the source of the credibility of what He reveals, the knowledge that is proper to faith also involves men giving their assent to divine testimony, namely, to *God* who makes himself known in what He reveals. In this singular faith-knowledge "the intellect and will exercise their spiritual character" by "fully and integrally accept[ing] the truth of things revealed, because *God offers himself* as their guarantee" (FeR §13, emphasis added).

The believer is certain that what is made known to us by revelation is true, *because* God is true, faithful, trustworthy, and himself the guarantor of that truth; not because the believer naturally sees its truth to be self-evident or can prove its truth.[31] In short, therefore, the doxastic practice of faith involves believing what God has revealed, because He has revealed it.[32]

Furthermore, the totally free gift of God's revealed truth "requires that it be accepted as a declaration of love" (FeR §13). The upshot here is summarily stated by John Henry Newman: "We believe because we love."[33] This declaration underscores the personalist character of faith in divine testimony.

Revelation and Authority

I will include here in this chapter on biblical authority an examination of the analysis of the relation between revelation and authority in G.C. Berkouwer's writings.[34] Berkouwer considers the question regarding the reasonableness of assenting to biblical authority. He explicitly resists the charge that "faith's response to God's revelation is nothing more than a *blind* submission, a *blind* trust without any insight into what is believed and accepted" (SI: 177-200, and at 177). On the one hand, Berkouwer holds that there is no place in our understanding of faith for sacrificing the intellect when that means eliminating human thought and insight. How, then, was the idea of sacrificing the intellect ever taken seriously, on the other?

Limiting myself to Catholic theology, in answering "the question *why* something is believed" a distinction is made in this tradition "between the motive of credibility (the reason for holding that the witness is sufficiently credible and that he in fact testifies to something) and the real motive of faith, that is, the sole authority of God, who is truth itself, incapable of deceiving anyone when he reveals himself."[35] In this light, we can answer Berkouwer's question why was the sacrifice of the intellect ever taken seriously.

The answer to this question is, briefly, that one believes on the authority of God the revealer and not on the basis of reason. So, then, on the other hand, "The answer to this question depends on the fact that in the arena of faith people did not intend to exclude all thought and reflection, but that they definitely did *not* want faith as accepting, embracing, and affirming the truth to depend on rational insight, but on the authority of revelation itself" (SI: 179-80). The point here is a familiar one, and Vatican I clearly makes it. Regarding the mysteries of faith, divine truths, such as the Trinity, the Incarnation, the Atoning Work of Christ, the Church, and so forth, the supernatural virtue of faith, which is the beginning of man's salvation, is required. "Whereby," the Dogmatic Decree of Vatican I adds, "inspired and assisted by the grace of God, we believe that the things which he has revealed are true; not because of the intrinsic truth of the things, viewed by the natural light of reason, but because of the authority of God himself, who reveals them, and who can neither be deceived nor deceive."[36] In other words, these truths are not evident to the intellect; they are true, we can know them to be true by faith, and the real ground of faith is the authority of the God who reveals himself.

The council approaches the question of faith accepting certain things to be true from the perspective of an authoritative revelation, upon which the acceptance of those truths is grounded. Says Berkouwer, "Submission can only be correlated with divine revelation. There can be no thought whatsoever of any critical verification in light of this *a priori* authority. The First Vatican Council expressed the matter in a way that made clear that people are entirely dependent on God and that their "*ratio creata*" is completely subordinate to eternal, uncreated truth" (SI: 181). The real ground and motive of the act of faith is the authority of the God who reveals himself and not the external motives of credibility that provides reasons for faith. The authority of God grounds the act of faith rather than being just one additional external motive of credibility. Brownsberger correctly notes, "The authority of God is that by which one believes, not that in consideration of which one believes."[37] Adds Berkouwer, "Faith is bound to revelation and submission and therein is faith's acceptance based on that alone, '*propter auctoritatem*'" (SI: 182).

Still, Berkouwer remarks critically that the problem of authority and reason is not resolved here because the Council decree states that the submission of faith to the authority of the revealing God is in *accordance with reason*. Yes, a Catholic theology of the act of faith holds that this act is essentially supernatural, but it is also reasonable. Clearly, then, the Council Fathers were concerned to legitimize—in avoidance of fideism—the credibility of the historical revelation of the Christian faith from the viewpoint of human reason. *Dei Filius* states the need for the external motives of credibility because "the assent of faith is by no means a blind impulse of the mind." Thus, "it was God's will that there should be linked to the internal assistance of the Holy Spirit external indications of his revelation, that is to say divine acts, and first and foremost miracles and prophecies, which clearly demonstrating as they do the omnipotence and infinite knowledge of God, are the most certain signs of revelation and are suited to the understanding of all."[38] The role of these exterior proofs or signs is that an historical apologetic establishes these signs of credibility as signs of God's revelation. What signs of credibility does the Council have in mind?

Well, clearly a miraculous event like the Resurrection of Jesus would count as a sign accrediting God's testimony. But how does one establish the judgment of credibility that this event is indeed a 'sign' as such provided by God's historical revelation? Although the Council decree leaves that question open, I venture to say that an historical apologetic would suffice that establishes the historicity of the events, such as the empty tomb, Jesus' post-mortem appearances, and the genesis of the disciples' belief that God had raised Jesus from the dead, as that which undergirds a historical inference to the historical fact of Jesus' resurrection.[39]

Of course these signs are facts bearing meaning, otherwise we would just have sheer facticity, and so the content of revelation to which they testify is itself the original theological meaning of the signs themselves. John Paul II explains, "These signs also urge reason to look beyond their status as signs in order to grasp the deeper meaning which they bear. They contain a hidden truth to which the mind is drawn and which it cannot ignore without destroying the very signs which it is given" (FeR §13). In sum, revelation presents the resurrection as a historical event with meta-historical meaning, to paraphrase Aidan Nichols.[40] Consider the description of event-plus-theological-intepretation, which is the wider significance inhering in the historical fact of Jesus' resurrection, given by St. Paul.

> Now if Christ is proclaimed as raised from the dead,
> how can some of you say that there is no resurrection
> of the dead? But if there is no resurrection of the dead,
> then not even Christ has been raised. And if Christ

has not been raised, then our preaching is in vain and your faith is in vain. We are even found to be misrepresenting God, because we testified about God that he raised Christ, whom he did not raise if it is true that the dead are not raised. For if the dead are not raised, not even Christ has been raised. And if Christ has not been raised, your faith is futile and you are still in your sins. Then those also who have fallen asleep in Christ have perished. If in Christ we have hope in this life only, we are of all people most to be pitied (1 Cor 15:12-19).

The question remains to be asked regarding the relation between the judgment of credibility and the act of faith. For to judge rationally that the historical events are credibly to be seen as signs of God's revelatory acts in history is "*not yet to make the act of supernatural faith.*"[41] "Faith is supernatural because it is only made possible by a supernatural interior grace."[42] Thus, there is also the necessity of the internal testimony of the Holy Spirit since "no man can assent to the Gospel teaching, as is necessary to obtain salvation, without the illumination and inspiration of the Holy Spirit, who gives to all men sweetness in assenting to and believing in the truth."[43] These two elements are, then, essential to the act of faith: the exterior sign and the interior grace by the testimony of the Holy Spirit. The epistemological significance of the Holy Spirit is not that this illumination and inspiration is an additional cognitive source of revealed truth. Rather, since the external motives of credibility on their own cannot move a person toward faith, the inward certainty regarding the truth of divine revelation is only accomplished by the Spirit of God "who moves us inwardly by his grace." As Aquinas explains: "Because it is not only exterior or objective revelation which has a power of attraction, but also the interior instinct impelling and moving me to belief, therefore the Father draws many to the Son by the interior instinct of the divine operation moving the heart of man to believe."[44]

The judgment of credibility regarding the external signs of revelation history belongs to the *praeambula fidei*. We may speak here of a 'historical faith' but not yet of 'saving faith.' There should be no opposition between these two. For of course the latter logically presupposes the former so that we can say that saving faith includes not only historical knowledge but also the saving knowledge that "if Christ has not been raised from the dead, my faith is futile and I am still in my sins" (1 Cor 15:18).

Now, Berkouwer rejects the claim that saving faith is *preceded* by "the preliminaries or presuppositions of faith" that here pertain, in the first place, to the historical faith that rests upon the judgment of credibility regarding the signs provided by the history of revelation and that accredit the testimony of revelation. "It is out of the question that there first has to be an act of *assensus* in which there is total assent—following historical verification, if necessary—to a kind of historical faith (*fides historica*) which would then expand into a saving faith (*fides salvifica*), and that the two together would then form the one Christian faith" (SI: 195).

In this passage, Berkouwer rejects the idea that the saving knowledge of God's acts in history is *preceded* by historical knowledge of the external signs of salvation history as preambles of faith. The point here is *not* that Berkouwer denies the fundamental significance of history for faith, say, that the resurrection actually happened in space and time. Rather, Berkouwer denies that faith rests upon historical evidence that establishes the historicity of the events, such as the empty tomb, Jesus' postmortem appearances, and the genesis of the disciples' belief that God had raised Jesus from the dead, as that which undergirds a historical inference to the historical fact of Jesus' resurrection, which then results in an acceptance of this fact, indeed, this "sign" of revelation history, that is called historical faith.

But how can the distinction between the resurrection "actually happened" and yet "cannot be grasped historically" be upheld?[45] It cannot be upheld. This is not because my acceptance of the resurrection would follow from my fashioning an historical apologetic that establishes the credibility of the signs of God's revelation. Rather, it is because the truth of the resurrection could not stand if it were definitely disproved that Jesus rose from the dead. It is the possibility of being open to falsification that we find the source of the believer's interest, as believer, in the external motives of credibility.[46]

Why does Berkouwer oppose the claim that the external signs of revelation history belong to the *praeambula fidei*? The answer to this question can be found in Berkouwer's theology of faith. He refers us to Lord's Day 7, Question 21, of the *Heidelberg Catechism*, which asks,

"What is true faith?" The answer that the *Catechism* gives is as follows: "True faith is not only a certain knowledge, whereby I hold for truth all that God has revealed to us in his word, (a) but also an assured confidence, (b) which the Holy Ghost (c) works by the gospel in my heart; (d) that not only to others, but to me also, remission of sin, everlasting righteousness and salvation, (e) are freely given by God, merely of grace, only for the sake of Christ's merits."[47] Berkouwer then remarks:

> The 'faith' in the prophets that Paul presupposes Agrippa has (Acts 26:27) is not *half* of that knowledge and trust concerning which the Catechism talks in explaining true faith. This acceptance is not an isolated pre-supposition of faith to which the '*pro nobis*' is then *added* as application. This is true because the 'informative' dimension itself of this knowledge is not given as an isolated 'announcement' of a brute fact, but as the disclosure of the meaning and inherent aspect of the saving event itself. So, the interpretation is not something added that factually ought not to be tied to the events themselves. Paul talks about the death of Christ *for our sins*—according to the Scriptures (1 Cor 15:3), so that one can say that people do not know the *fact*—in an act of assenting, accepting—if they separate or isolate it from this aspect (SI: 196-97).

Berkouwer's theology of faith consists of knowledge (*notitia*), assent (*assensus*), and trust (*fiducia*). The issue here is *not* that Berkouwer denies that the Christian faith rests on the truth of a historical revelation, of events that actually happened, with the act of faith involving, logically if not temporally, assenting (*assensus*), knowledge (*notitia*) and acceptance of certain historical truths. Rather, the issue is that this approach that distinguishes historical faith from saving faith results in the treatment of the signs of credibility as essentially extrinsically related to the content of revelation to which they testify.

In other words, a judgment of credibility, according to Berkouwer, leaves us with historical information of 'brute facts,' meaning thereby facts without significance. Berkouwer rejects the extraneous nature of this connection between historical judgment and the act of faith that makes possible the knowledge that the revelation is itself the inherent meaning of the signs, what the signs signify. Since the revelation is itself the significance of the signs, we cannot know the fact of Jesus' resurrection without seeing its intrinsic relation to that revelation.

> Whenever faith is considered as assent, knowledge, and holding something to be true, it is impossible to isolate or highlight these aspects in abstraction from the central reality of the heart's assent. Without this central reality, acceptance, assent, holding something to be true, loses its specifically Christian character. Christian faith is only rightly understood in terms of the connection between the informative and inherent meaning of saving events because this is the way the gospel's call is extended to people—one could say as assent, adherence, cognition, trust, and obedience (SI: 195-96).

But it seems to me that Berkouwer misunderstands the external motives of credibility. The historical judgment purports to establish, not only that events such as the resurrection actually happened, brute facts as it were, but also that they are indeed 'signs' of credibility regarding revelation history to which they testify. In other words, these signs of credibility establish not only "the historical actuality of the fact of revelation" but also "the meaning of its content."[48] So they are not in danger of losing their specifically Christian meaning, as Berkouwer suggests in the above quotation. Yes, *pace* Berkouwer, it is historical reason which initially established the status of these events as signs, and not just as things that merely happened—though one must not underestimate the value of this historical evidence for faith—but "these signs also urge reason to look beyond their status as signs in order to grasp the deeper meaning which they bear." "They contain a hidden truth to which the mind is drawn," John Paul II adds, "and which it cannot ignore without destroying the very signs which it is given" (FeR §13). This, too, is Berkouwer's point in the above quotation. But unlike Berkouwer, John Paul thinks—in line with Vatican I and II—that we can show that the act of faith is reasonable because of the external motives of credibility: there is historical evidence for the resurrection of Jesus.

For Berkouwer faith's knowledge of the resurrection is "excluded altogether from the domain of proof, of evidence and hence of rationality."[49] But Berkouwer cannot consistently posit such a break between faith's knowledge that something actually happened and historical evidence regarding the resurrection, since if that knowledge is making assertions about objective reality, as he surely holds it is, then, it must be open to falsification by historical evidence. Hence, the import of using historical evidence to build a reasonable case supporting a judgment of credibility that we have here a sign provided by revelation history.

Positivism of Revelation?

There is another reason to consider why Berkouwer opposes the external motives of credibility. He understands that the grounds of credibility do not prove faith itself but rather establish its credibility by showing that the consent to faith is reasonable. Berkouwer gives a clear explanation as to why the external motives of credibility do not bring into question the authority of God himself. He writes:

> Vatican I also concludes from this "*propter [auctoritatem ipsius Dei revelantis]*" against holding to *blind* faith, but involves itself with the issue of the why of faith. Certainly, God's authority as '*summe verax*' [perfectly truthful] is of decisive significance. But granted this genesis of faith, people then go on to reflect on the credibility of revelation [motives of credibility]. In other words, they go on to reflect on the nature and content of revelation and its illuminating power within the horizon of human existence. In this way, one can distinguish between the actual foundation for faith (divine authority) and the issue of *faith's credibility* that does play a role in believing. People cannot rest completely on the concept of formal authority ["*propter auctoritatem ipsius Dei revelantis*"], arriving automatically at a closer reflection on the necessity for 'the light of faith' that in turn produces acceptance of divine revelation. Rather, in their concrete situation, people realize that they are confronted with a unique authority that calls them to make a definite choice.[50]

Now, since supernatural faith does not rest on human testimony of the judgments of credibility but rather on divine testimony, namely, the authority of the God who reveals himself, the question raised by this view of divine authority as expressed by Vatican I, says Berkouwer, is that the assent of faith seems "severed from the content of the message of salvation: it has no inner affinity with this message."[51] Yes, the decree makes clear that there are motives of credibility showing that the "assent of faith is by no means a blind action of the mind." These motives of credibility establish the rationality of believing and hence the credibility of these signs as God's revelation. But those motives only justify the reasonableness of believing *that* something has been revealed and *why* it should be believed, in short, its formal authority; they do not provide, however, an 'inner conviction' regarding *what* has been revealed, its material authority, namely, "the object and content of faith to which man is called" (HS, II, 419 [349]). Berkouwer is raising here an objection that held the attention of some of the best minds in Catholic theology of the early twentieth century (Maurice Blondel, Ambroise Gardeil, and Pierre Rousselot), namely, the "signs of credibility seem essentially extraneous to the revelation to which they testify."[52] Consequently, Berkouwer argues, faith is, then, reduced to the act of assenting to the truths that must be blindly believed and accepted on authority.

This is a treacherous route, he claims, not because the authority of God and of his revelation has an inappropriate significance in the correlation between faith and revelation, but rather "the formal and material authority of revelation are separated, and faith is placed in the framework of an abstract acceptance of authority" (SI: 188). *Deus dixit*, and that settles it. Berkouwer's critique of Vatican I focuses on what he regards, following Dietrich Bonhoeffer (1906-1945), as a *positivism of revelation* and the corresponding act of faith, understood as the mere assent and acceptance of incomprehensible and equally significant truths, "a necessary part of the whole, which must simply be swallowed as a whole or not at all."[53] Throughout his post-1968 writings Berkouwer often cites Bonhoeffer's critique of Karl Barth's "revelation positivism."[54] What is the point of this criticism?

> Now, whenever Bonhoeffer talks about the "positivism of revelation," a conception of faith is indicated—resulting in the dogmatic methodology—in which various "truths" are accepted on the basis of *revelation* and not on the basis of ecclesial authority. . . . In *this* sort

of faith-appropriation, according to Bonhoeffer, '*ein Gesetz der Glaubens*' is created: one is *simply compelled* to accept various truths. In this critique, Bonhoeffer is concerned about not only a dogmatic view of 'the faith,' but also sees in the positivism of revelation—embracing a number of revealed truths in a leveling manner—the positing of a world that is left to itself; "*das ist ihr Fehler*" because *that* kind of embracing of truths does not involve the *world* with which it is *immediately* and *actually* connected. . . . A dualism arises that can no longer find a way to the world. . . . In the background of Bonhoeffer's critique there is a leveling 'acceptance' of the truths of revelation without the "*Stufen der Erkenntnis un Stufen der Bedeutsamkeit*" ["substance of discernment and the substance of meaning"], and therefore, on the basis of *the quality of such authority*, may not be doubted or questioned. Bonhoeffer sees *such* truths obviously functioning as impediments, as stumbling blocks. Here there is no thought of understanding *meaning* and therefore of a direction giving relatedness to such truths. The "*propter auctoritatem [ipsius Dei revelantis]*" is in danger of becoming purely formal because an understanding of the truth is erased, and faith assumes the function of 'accepting truths,' that is, faith as *assent* (SI: 192-93).

In the above passage, Berkouwer is arguing that the view of authority represented by Vatican I is a heteronomous view of authority with a corresponding authoritarian view of faith. "At issue is the notion of faith as an assent to certain truths. We are dealing with a concept of faith that makes the object of faith heteronomous, foreign to man's nature, and remaining foreign while one keeps believing."[55] In short, faith on the basis of authority seems to leave us, Berkouwer adds, with a "formal authority that can and must be believed no matter what words are spoken" (HS, II, 424 [353]). We are left, then—and this is the upshot of Berkouwer's critique of this authoritarian view of faith—with truth being understood as an "irrational 'foreign body' in the world, without "testifying, appellative, and verifying force."[56]

Berkouwer's problem is not that some people "speak of the authority of God and of the definitive meaning of his revelation, but rather that they separate the formal and material ["content"] authority of revelation and then place faith in a framework where it is taken to mean acceptance of authority isolated from the content of revelation" (HS, II, 424 [353]). Berkouwer, therefore, concludes that this view of biblical authority leaves us with a mere formal authority, a heteronomous power, or as Dietrich Bonhoeffer once put it, a "positivist doctrine of revelation which says, in effect, 'Like it or lump it',"[57] whereby man is reduced by God's Word ("*Deus dixit*") to passivity, blind submission, and in which a concept of faith is rendered as a sacrifice of the intellect, blind faith, not allowing any insight, understanding, or response on man's part. Berkouwer is right that this view entails a "dangerous view of faith" (HS, II, 422 [352]). The only question is whether his critique of Vatican I is accurate, namely, that basing faith's knowledge of God on authority is heteronomous.

Let me be clear that Berkouwer is not questioning Vatican I's emphasis on God's authority. In other words, he, too, holds that theological faith is based on that authority as its ultimate motive and formal object. Berkouwer's position on authority and experience does not imply a "subjectification of authority, which might only become reality through acknowledgment."[58] Rather, "faith is not founded on human reliability but on the explicit authority of God himself, the deep foundation of all apostolic authority" (HS, II, 419 [349]).

Let me also make it clear that Berkouwer does not reject a propositional view of faith—as long as we do not understand faith *first and last* to mean only holding certain propositions to be true, then Berkouwer has no difficulty taking the act of "faith's assent-function to mean that it must believe and accept certain truths" (SI: 188). Says Berkouwer, "There is no reason to reject the words 'assent', 'acceptance', or 'hold to be true.' All these terms are meaningful and legitimate as long as they are maintained in the right framework, which is to say as long as they are not separated from the content of revelation" (ibid.). Put differently, Berkouwer agrees (in my own terms) that theological faith involves holding certain propositions to be true, holding them to be divinely revealed, and holding them because we believe God who reveals them. In short, faith therefore believes what is revealed because of who reveals it.

Still, Berkouwer objects to Vatican I's view of authority because it bases faith's knowledge of God on authority, and on this view the object and content of faith is heteronomous. "For faith," says Berkouwer, "would then be called to a decision without inner conviction regarding the object and content of the faith to which man is called." Berkouwer seeks to counteract this view of God's authority by arguing that "this authority does not exclude experience and man is freely part of it; but *in* the experience the authority is acknowledged and confessed. Scriptural faith is part of this acknowledgment and is manifested in submission and the obedience of faith" (HS, II, 419 [349]).

Elsewhere he expresses the correlation between faith and understanding to be such that this correlation is grounded in the unique authority of Scripture rather than in that view in which this authority is made to rest on man's insight and understanding, which results in the subjectification of biblical authority (SI: 198). He adds, "It is the deep dynamic of faith in the authority of Scripture that is daily confirmed *in* understanding and *in* listening." This deep dynamic of faith involves "a faithful listening—*ex auditu Verbi*—that more deeply understands what it hears and therein finds rest" (ibid.).

In this biblical vision, faith is never and nowhere portrayed as an irrational acceptance of the objective content of faith on the basis of authority, whereby the emphasis is more on the "that" than the "what" of revelation. Rather, says Berkouwer, "Revelation may never even for a moment be abstracted from the self-revealing God." Indeed, God's gift of himself in revelation involves man "being called to his communion, called to walking in his way, to a faithful listening to his Word. Without this context, faith loses its deepest meaning" (SI: 187). In God's calling humanity to faith, he is called to be "transformed by the renewing of [his] mind" (Rom 12:2).

In other words, faith's acceptance of biblical authority means that he "is persuaded [to respond to the Gospel] through the reality of the proclaimed content of the gospel so that he is not led to a sacrifice of the intellect but to renewal of his thought (Rom 12:2), born in the freedom of faith and issuing in gratitude and adoration. We are dealing here with a faith that is not subject to rational yardsticks and needs no approval of rational verification and yet cannot be separated from insight. . . . This faith is no less full of certainty" (HS, II, 422 [352-53]). But what then is the ground of faith's certainty?

Well, given the distinction between the real ground and motive of faith on the one hand, and the grounds of credibility on the other, we already know that faith's certainty is not derived from the latter. Berkouwer recognizes this distinction's importance in Vatican I's theology of faith. But he charges the Council with a heteronomous view of faith, namely, "faith on the basis of *authority*."[59] Berkouwer charges that this is a positivist doctrine of revelation's authority, which says, in effect, "Like it or lump it." Walter Cardinal Kasper has rightly questioned this interpretation of *Dei Filius* of Vatican I. He writes:

> The Constitution [*Dei Filius*] speaks not of *auctoritas Dei imperantis* [God's commanding authority], but of *auctoritas Dei revelantis* [authority of God revealing]. It is not, in other words, a question of pure authority as such. We are not told that God has revealed something and that is that. This kind of [revelation] positivism with regard to faith and this kind of obedience are not in accordance with the teaching of the Church. The certainty of faith is rather based in the evidence and authority of the truth of God. This means that problems of faith cannot be reduced—as they often are nowadays—to problems of obedience. We do not, then, believe the Church. We believe because we are convinced of the truth of the God who reveals himself.[60]

Kasper is correctly arguing in this passage that the problem with Berkouwer's interpretation is his understanding of how a person believes on the authority of God. I agree with William Brownsberger that the Council did not "close off discussion about how this authority is to be understood."[61] As Berkouwer himself rightly remarks, "We must not get caught up in an emotional reaction against such phrases as 'believing on authority'. Everything depends on the character of the authority and the character of believing."[62] I will now argue that we can best understand the nature of this authority and the corresponding act of faith in terms of an epistemology of testimony in order to rebut Berkouwer's charge that Vatican I's view of authority is heteronomous. Pared down for my purpose here, I will sketch an account of testimony's role in the acquisition of knowledge, showing that authority is not a "darksome power that compels us to subject ourselves without reason."[63]

In the concluding sentence of the above quotation of Kasper, he claims that we believe a statement to be true, and hence possess the certainty of faith, "because we are convinced of the truth of the God who reveals himself." What does this conviction mean? In other words, what convinces us of the truth of the God who reveals himself? Well, it cannot be that I see for myself the truth of the statements to be believed. Rather, we believe because of the authority of the God who reveals himself. This means that God himself is the source of the credibility of what he reveals and that he is thereby the guarantor of that truth. (FeR §13)

What accounts then for our conviction of credibility? Mouroux answers this question: "we *meet* with a person—that explains the certainty of faith."[64] In other words, with faith I accept the truth of what God says about Himself, and in doing so I not only share in His self-knowledge but also accept the Person who reveals Himself through His divine testimony. This statement brings us back to testimonial knowledge and the role of testimony in acquiring such knowledge.

This fundamental question is about whether each man should confine himself to what he knows in virtue of what he could in principle find out directly for himself by means of personal experience, insights, and grasp of the truth without relying on anyone else for acquiring knowledge.[65] As Paul Helm asks, "Besides the things which we get to know for ourselves, are there not many things for which we must rely on others? What about the testimony of others?"[66] Aquinas already answered Helm's question regarding human testimony by arguing that human faith, meaning thereby trust in another, is necessary.

> And because in human society one person must make use of another just as he does himself in matters in which he is not self-sufficient, he must take his stand on what another knows and is unknown to himself, just as he does on what he himself knows. Consequently, faith is necessary in human society, one person believing what another says.[67]

Elsewhere Aquinas writes in the same vein: "If one were willing to believe only those things which one knows with certitude, one could not live in this world. How could one live unless one believed others? How could one know that this man is one's own father? Therefore, it is necessary that one believes others in matters which one cannot know perfectly of oneself."[68] One person believing what another says, trusting the word of another, involves an element of participating and sharing the knowledge of another.

What is the meaning here of believing what another says, particularly with respect to sharing in the testimonial knowledge of the Bible? Trusting in the word of another by which I participate and share in his knowledge is true of virtually all knowledge, scientific, historical, moral, theological, and many others.[69]

In the case of acquiring knowledge through the testimony of God in his written Word revelation, here, too, credibility is not separated from testimony. Here, too, I share in God's knowledge that comes to me from others, but this sharing in the knowledge of another "is more personal than the knowledge I share with the technician or specialist" (C&CC, 103). As John Paul rightly notes, "In knowing by faith, man accepts the whole supernatural and salvific content of revelation as true. But at the same time, this fact introduces him into a profound personal relationship with God who reveals Himself" (CoC §44).

Therefore, our knowledge of God is essentially based on faith, on a trust that is participatory of "what another has *seen*" (C&CC, 104). Ratzinger explains, "Christ is there, at the very center of history, as the great man who sees, and all his words flow from his immediate contact with the Father.

As for us, the word that refers to our situation is: 'He who has seen *me* has seen the Father' (John 14:9). In its innermost essence, the Christian faith is a participation in this act whereby Jesus *sees*. His act of seeing makes possible his word, which is the authentic expression of what he sees. Accordingly, what Jesus sees is the point of reference for our faith, the specific place where it is anchored" (C&CC, 104-105). Ratzinger's point that our faith is anchored in what Jesus *sees* brings us back to the question regarding the certainty of faith.

What, then, explains the certainty of faith? "Faith is certain, and thus I am sure of possessing what is true; yet I do not see it."[70] In other words, I do not see for myself the truth of statements, such as "And the Word became flesh and dwelt among us, and we have seen his glory, glory as of the only Son from the Father, full of grace and truth" (John 1:14). "Why then am I sure?" Mouroux insightfully replies by appealing to what another has *seen*. "Through Christ, our connection with God is assured":

> Because I am united to Someone who sees. Faith is certain, not because it comprises the *evidence of a thing seen*, but because it is the *assent to a Person who sees*. This is just what we would expect. If the essential in faith is not primarily the fragmentary truths, but the person to whom we tend through these truths—"Him to whose word we assent"—it is quite clear that our certitude will be based on this Person. For it is this Person, and he alone, who sees the truths, and who can therefore give our knowledge a solid foundation. As St. Thomas puts it in an extremely precise formula: the full affirmation does not proceed from the vision of the believer, but from the vision of Him in Whom one believes, *non procedit ex visione credentis, sed a visione ejus cui creditur* [*Summa Theologiae*, 1a, q. xii, a. 13, ad. 3; cf. Summa Contra Gentiles, 111, 154, init.], Faith is an assent to the First Truth, that is to an Infallible Person.[71]

Lastly, *pace* Berkouwer, this act of faith is not heteronomous because it essentially involves the "act of entrusting oneself to God," of the gift of giving oneself, meaning thereby a "fundamental decision which engages the whole person."[72] Hence, in the act of faith I become a sharer in the knowledge of God that comes to me from the divine testimony of his Word. This is not a *blind* faith, a *blind* trust, a leap in the dark; no, it is a form of knowledge, not merely involving an assent to the truth of a proposition, but also *"the person to whose words the assent is given,"*[73] resulting in a personal knowledge containing an element of participation, where by means of trusting God, I share in his knowledge, in the knowledge of the Person *who sees*, and by God's grace I am permitted *to see*. Thus, in conclusion:

> When we put our confidence in what Jesus sees and believes in his word, we are not in fact moving around in total darkness. The good news of Jesus corresponds to an interior expectation in our heart; it corresponds to an internal light in our being that reaches out to the truth of God. Certainly, we are before all else believers

"at second hand." But Saint Thomas is right to describe faith as a process, as an interior path, when he writes: "The light of faith leads us to see." [For] in the living encounter with [Jesus Christ], faith is transformed into "knowledge" (C&CC, 110-11).

Yet faith's knowledge is not the kind of knowledge that has no more questions. Faith's knowledge is such that it possesses an inherent dynamism toward seeking understanding of the truth that we have grasped. This is the dynamic of faith seeking understanding. Ratzinger correctly adds, "It would of course be wrong to imagine the subsequent path of faith as a linear process, as an untrammeled development" (C&CC, 111). This point is particularly important given the heartbreak, grief, and suffering that my family and I experience with the death of our beloved Penny. Again, Ratzinger is right: "Since this path is linked to our life with all its ups and downs, we keep experiencing setbacks that oblige us to start anew." Furthermore, then, "Every phase of life has to discover its own specific maturity, for otherwise we fall back into corresponding immaturity. And yet, we can say that the life of faith also permits the growth of an evidential character of the faith: its reality touches us, and the experience of a successful life of faith assures us that Jesus is truly the Savior of the world" (ibid.) That is my conviction as I turn to discuss the evidential character of faith in light of the interplay between faith and reason.

Notes

1. Joseph Ratzinger, *Introduction to Christianity*, 296, 310, respectively.

2. St. Thomas Aquinas, *Summa Theologica*, II-II, q. 2, a. 4.

3. On the defense of this claim regarding the legitimacy of theistic arguments, see William Lane Craig, "God is not Dead Yet," Christianity Today, July 2008, 22-27; "http://www.reasonablefaith.org/god-is-not-dead-yet. See also, "The New Atheism and Five Arguments for God," http://www.reasonablefaith.org/the-new-atheism-and-five-arguments-for-god.

4. "Agnosticism," in *Routledge Encyclopedia of Philosophy*.

5. William James, "The Will to Believe" (1896) in *The Will to Believe and other essays in popular philosophy*, 1-31. Charles Taylor, *Varieties of Religion Today: William James Revisited*, has a particularly important discussion of James's critique of agnosticism, 42-60.

6. Ibid. Elsewhere in the essay, "The Sentiment of Rationality," James makes a simi-

lar point about "forced option": "If this really be a moral universe; if by acts I be a factor of its destinies; if to believe where I may doubt be itself a moral act analogous to voting for a side not yet sure to win—by what right shall they close in upon me and steadily negate the deepest conceivable function of my being by their preposterous command that I shall stir neither hand nor foot, but remain balancing myself in eternal and insoluble doubt? Why, doubt itself is a decision of the widest practical reach, if only because we may miss by doubting what goods we night be gaining by espousing the winning side. But more than that! It is often practically impossible to distinguish doubt from dogmatic negation. If I refuse to stop a murder because I am in doubt whether it is not justifiable homicide, I am virtually abetting the crime. If I refuse to bale out a boat because I am in doubt whether my efforts will keep her afloat, I am really helping to sink her. . . . Scepticism in moral matters is an active ally of immorality. Who is not for is against. The universe will have no neutrals in these questions. In theory as in practice, dodge or hedge, or talk as we like about a wise scepticism, we are really doing volunteer service for one side or the other" (108-9).

7. Taylor, *Varieties of Religion Today*, 48.

8. Ibid., 49.

9. Alvin Plantinga, *Warranted Christian Belief*,147, 251-52, 266-67. I borrow the apt phrase "modest testimonial foundationalism" from Kevin Vanhoozer, *Biblical Authority After Babel*, 72. I am drawing here on some material from my book, *Revelation, History, and Truth: A Hermeneutics of Dogma*, chapter 3.

10. Helm, *Faith, Form, and Fashion*, 218.

11. Wahlberg, *Revelation as Testimony*, 126.

12. For an important defense of revelation as testimony and hence of the rationality of testimonial knowledge, see Wahlberg, *Revelation as Testimony*, 124-43.

13. John Henry Newman, Sermon XV, 194.

14. Anscombe, "What is it to Believe Someone," 143.

15. Newman, Sermon XV, 194.

16. Thomas Aquinas states, "Other things being equal, sight is more certain than hearing; but if (the authority) of the persons from whom we hear greatly surpasses that of the seer's sight, hearing is more certain than sight . . . and much more is a man certain about what he hears from God who cannot be deceived, than about what he sees with his own reason which can be mistaken" (Thomas Aquinas, *Summa Theologica*, IIa, IIae, q.4, a.8. ad.2; http://www.newadvent.org/summa/).

17. Anscombe shares this view: "The greater part of our knowledge of reality rests upon the belief that we repose in things that we have been taught and told" ("What is it to Believe Someone," 143). So, too, does Aquinas: 'And because in human society one person must make use of another just as he does himself in matters in which he is not self-sufficient, he must take his stand on what another knows and is unknown to himself, just as he does on what he himself knows. As a consequence, faith is necessary in human society, one person believing what another says' (Aquinas 1987 [1259], q.3, a.1, reply, 65-66). And this, too, is the view of Ratzinger, *Christianity and the Crisis of Cultures*, 79-82.

18. Newman, Sermon XV, 195. Newman uses the Old English word "fain" meaning thereby amenable, disposed, willing, game, glad, inclined, minded, and ready.

19. Newman, Sermon XV, 195.

20. J.L.A. Garcia, "Moral Reasoning & the Catholic Church," 16.

21. Vanhoozer, "Hermeneutics of I-Witness Testimony," 269.

22. Garcia, "Moral Reasoning & the Catholic Church," 14.

23. Ibid.

24. Linda Zagzebski, "A Modern Defense of Religious Authority," 21.

25. Newman, Sermon XV, 196. So, too, Ratzinger, *C&CC*, 103.

26. Plantinga, *Knowledge and Christian Belief,* 46.

27. Mouroux, *I Believe: The Personal Structure of Faith*, 17.

28. Vanhoozer, *Biblical Authority After Babel*, 98.

29. Aquinas, *Summa Theologica*, II-II, q.11, a.1.

30. Ibid., q.129, a.6.

31. It would take us too far afield to discuss the epistemological significance of the Church's authority and the nature and extent of ecclesial authority. The question of ecclesial authority is connected with the wider issues of theological epistemology because the Church also holds assertoric authority when it teaches authoritatively in matters of faith and morals under the presumed guidance of the Holy Spirit.

32. As Vatican I was to put it in 1869 in its Dogmatic Constitution *Dei Filius*: 'We believe [by faith] that what he has revealed is true, not because the intrinsic truth of things is recognized by the natural light of reason, but because of the authority of God himself who reveals them, who can neither err nor deceive' (Heinrich Denzinger, *Compendium of Creeds, Definitions, and Declarations on Matters of Faith and Morals*, §§2012, 3008).

33. John Henry Newman, "Love the Safeguard of Faith Against Superstition," Sermon XII, *Oxford University Sermons*, preached on Whit Sunday (21 May 1839), http://www.newmanreader.org/works/oxford/serman12.html.

34. This section on revelation and authority is adapted from Chapter 3 of my book, *Berkouwer and Catholicism, Disputed Questions* and from a later version, "Revelation and Authority: Preamble of Faith and an Epistemology of Testimony," 18-28.

35. Rahner, and Vorgrimler. *Theological Dictionary*, 168.

36. Vatican I, 1870, *Decreta Dogmatica Concilii Vaticani de Fide Catholica et de Ecclesia Christi*, Chapter III, *Of Faith*, Chapter 4. See Denzinger, §3020.

37. Brownsberger, "The Authority of God and the Act of Faith," 156.

38. Vatican Council I, *Dei Filius*, Chapter 3, *On Faith*, §5. See also the First Vatican Council canon 3, *de fide*: "If anyone says that divine revelation cannot be made credible by external signs and that therefore men should be drawn only by their personal internal experience or by private inspiration, let him be anathema."

39. William Lane Craig, "Did Jesus Rise from the Dead?" in *Jesus Under Fire*, 142-176; idem., "Dale Allison on Jesus' Empty Tomb, his Postmortem Appearances,

and the Origin of the Disciples Belief in his resurrection," 293-301.

40. Nichols, *Epiphany: A Theological Introduction to Catholicism*, 176.

41. Idem, *From Hermes to Benedict XVI*,183.

42. Rahner and Vorgrimler, *Theological Dictionary*, 168.

43. *Dei Filius*, 244.

44. St. Thomas Aquinas, *In Ioannem* c.vi, lect. 5, §3, as cited in Mouroux, 21.

45. Roger Trigg, "Can a Religion Rest on Historical Claims," in *Rationality and Religion*, 91-112, and for these phrases, 94.

46. Ralph McInerny, "Philosophizing in Faith," 244.

47. *Heidelberg Catechism*, 1563, Lord's Day 7, Question 21.

48. Nichols, *From Hermes to Benedict XVI*, 187. As Germain Grisez explains, "revelation also requires a distinctive signal; it must include elements—words and deeds—which cannot reasonably be interpreted as anything except divine communication. This is to say that it necessarily includes signs and wonder: states of affairs brought about by God without the usual conditions which, if present, would dispose people to regard these happenings as part of the normal course of events" (*The Way of the Lord Jesus*, I, *Christian Moral Principles*, 479-80).

49. Trigg, "Can a Religion Rest on Historical Claims," 98.

50. Berkouwer, "Sacrificium Intellectus?" 182. "Because of the authority of the revealing God" is the meaning of "*propter auctoritatem ipsius Dei revelantis.*"

51. HS, II, 422 [352]. Berkouwer is not directing his critical remarks against Vatican I's view of divine authority. Rather, he is questioning a notion of formal authority (*why* something is believed) that is separated from material authority (*what* is believed).

52. Nichols, *From Hermes to Benedict XVI*, 187. Nichols give an instructive account of how Catholic thinkers from Blondel to Balthasar dealt with that objection in chapter 9, "The Dispute over Apologetics: From Blondel to Balthasar," 173-96.

53. Berkouwer, *Een Halve Eeuw Theologie*, 219 [155].

54. Berkouwer, "Sacrificium Intellectus?" 192-93, 196; idem., "De Achtergrond," 13; idem., *Een Halve Eeuw Theologie*, [155].

55. Berkouwer, *Een Halve Eeuw Theologie, Een Halve Eeuw Theologie, Motieven en Stromingen van 1920 to Heden* (Kampen: J.H. Kok, 1974), 220. ET: *A Half Century of Theology: Movements and Motives*, translated and edited by Lewis B. Smedes (Grand Rapids, MI: Eerdmans, 1977), 156. Both sources will be cited in this article, first the original, followed by the pagination of the English in square brackets [ ].

56. Berkouwer, De Achtergrond," In: *De Herleving van de Natuurlijke Theologie*. Kampen: J.H. Kok, 1974, 3-17, and at 16.

57. Bonhoeffer, *Letters and Papers from Prison*, 157. Bonhoeffer actually said in German, "frisz, Vogel ober stirb!," which literally translated mean, "Eat, bird or die." This is taken to express the authoritarian call that "alle 'openbaarde waarheden' op gezag *aan te nemen*" ["all revealed truth should be accepted on authority"]

(Berkouwer, "Achtergrond," 13). Hendrikus Berkhof writes that Bonhoeffer's "words about Barth's 'positivism of revelation' ('Take it or leave it') struck like a bomb. These words were exceedingly painful to Barth. One can say that the post-Barthian period really starts with the publication of this position of Bonhoeffer. It arose directly from his analysis of the new cultural epoch. In the anthropocentric age in which Barth had sought his way as a theologian, his starting with God as the subject of faith and theology was a liberating new beginning. In Bonhoeffer's time this point had already become self-evident in theology. But in the period which he foresaw, such a starting point would be completely unintelligible. For the people for whom the working hypothesis 'God' would be a total redundancy, 'the authority of the Word of God' would only constitute a double enigma: first, because they would accept nothing on authority anymore and, second, because they could not handle the idea of 'speaking God'. Since Bonhoeffer's time countless preachers, pastoral-care workers, and theologians experienced that they had to work under these conditions and –whatever they may have believed and thought for themselves—found themselves unable to start in their work where Barth did" (*Two Hundred Years of Theology*, Translated by John Vriend [Grand Rapids, Michigan: Eerdmans], 1989, 209-10).

58. Berkouwer, HS, II, 418 [348]. It is hard to see how Francis Schüssler Fiorenza avoids the "subjectification of authority" in the following statement of his position in his 1987 Presidential Address to the Catholic Theological Society of America ("Foundations of Theology," 107-34) regarding the authority of divine revelation. He rejects the approach to revelation and faith that emphasizes "the authority of revelation and the relation of this authority to the truthfulness of God." He holds, instead, that "the authority of revelation is an authority that needs to be gained through the interpretation of what is revelation" (114).

59. Berkouwer, *Een Halve Eeuw Theologie*, 220 [156].

60. Kasper, *Introduction to Christian Faith*, 63.

61. Brownsberger, "The Authority of God and the Act of Faith," 160n45.

62. Berkouwer, *Een Halve Eeuw Theologie*, 224 [159].

63. Ibid., 223 [158].

64. Mouroux, *I Believe*, 59.

65. Lonergan develops this question in his, *Insight, A Study...*, 703-6.

66. Helm, *Faith and Understanding*, 19.

67. Thomas Aquinas, *Faith, Reason and Theology*, Questions 1-4 of his *Commentary on the De Trinitate of Boethius*, Q. 3, art. 1, 65-66.

68. Thomas Aquinas, *The Catechetical Instruction of St. Thomas Aquinas*, 4.

69. Swinburne, *Faith and Reason*, 40-43.

70. Mouroux, *I Believe*, 54.

71. Ibid., 54-55.

72. John Paul II, *Fides et Ratio*, "This is why the Church has always considered the act of entrusting oneself to God to be a moment of fundamental decision which engages the whole person. In that act, the intellect and the will display their spiritual

nature, enabling the subject to act in a way which realizes personal freedom to the full" (§13). See also, Pius XII, *Humani Generis*, §§32-33.

73. Thomas Aquinas, *Summa Theologiae*, IIa, IIae, q. xi, a.1.

CHAPTER 2

The Problem of Evil and Suffering

The believing philosopher should not hesitate to include the redemptive vision of his faith in his speculation.[1]

Advice to Christian Philosophers

In his 1962 intellectual autobiography, *The Philosopher and Theology*, Catholic philosopher, neo-Thomist Étienne Gilson wrote regarding the future of Christian philosophy: "The necessary condition to insure the future of Christian philosophy is to maintain the primacy of the Word of God, *even in philosophical inquiry*." "I am tempted to say," adds Gilson, "above all in matters of philosophical speculation."[2]

We find a similar accent on the primacy of God's Word in philosophical inquiry almost four decades later in John Paul II's *Fides et Ratio* (FeR §§80-89). This philosopher-pope affirms the notion of Christian philosophy, which is, according to John Paul, "the art of philosophizing in a Christian manner; namely a philosophical reflection [and practice] that is vitally conjoined to faith" (FeR §76).[3] In this connection, most significant is John Paul's commitment to, and call for, a scripturally-based philosophy, a Christian philosophy, one consonant with the Word of God itself, which one may never neglect without impunity. "In refusing the truth offered by divine revelation, philosophy only does itself damage, since this is to cut off access to a deeper knowledge of the truth" (FeR §75). One important example of this revelation-based approach to truth is knowledge of "the reality of sin, as it appears in the light of faith, which helps to shape an adequate philosophical formulation of the problem of evil" (FeR §76). The pope's claim requires some explanation.

John Paul II's reflections on the meaning of human suffering in his Apostolic Letter *Salvifici Doloris*[4] do not start from a religiously neutral position. Rather, his starting point is a set of beliefs that are "life-orienting beliefs" because they shape and direct your thoughts and actions throughout your life.[5] Thus, this philosopher-Pope undoubtedly thinks it perfectly appropriate, in philosophical enquiry, to appeal to what he knows by way of faith. Let me make it clear that it is not that John Paul leaves questions about God, evil, and suffering entirely in the hands of faith. Indeed not, since philosophical argument and analysis assists the teachings of faith by sketching some traditional arguments suggesting that the idea of a God infinite in knowledge, goodness, and power is compatible with the actual existence of evil. In other words, John Paul accepts philosophical reason's modest yet legitimate demand, in Louis Dupré's words, "to perceive how an open conflict between a good God and an evil world is *not inevitable*."[6]

Yet the pope agrees, I think, with Dupré, who writes: "The very standards by which we measure what does and what does not count as 'good' depend upon the acceptance or rejection of an intrinsically religious hierarchization of values. Any attempt to erect a system of values upon a religiously neutral basis, common to believers and unbelievers, fails precisely in the area where theodicy matters most, namely in deciding what must count as *definitive* evil." "Varying ontological commitments," adds Dupré, "widen or narrow the range of options for defeating evil with good.'"[7] Such value-theory pluralism justifies Christians to let revelation-based truth enter the domain of reason, says Maritain, "bringing along the help of a light and a truth which are superior, and which elevate reason in its own order—that is what happens with Christian philosophy."[8]

Indeed, John Paul II affirms that "revealed truth offers the fullness of light and will therefore illumine the path of philosophical inquiry" (FeR §79). Accordingly, engaging the data of revelation has enriched philosophical inquiry. Philosophical reason "is offered guidance and is warned against paths which would lead it to stray from revealed Truth and to stray in the end from the truth pure and simple." But the influence of faith is not exercised purely as a negative norm, as though

Christian philosophers strive in their theorizing merely not to contradict the faith (FeR §63). "Instead," the pope adds, "reason is stirred to explore paths which of itself would not even have suspected it could take. This relationship with the word of God leaves philosophy enriched, because reason discovers new and unsuspected horizons" (FeR §73). Indeed, faith should have a positive influence on philosophical reflection.

Most important, the pope not only accepts the concept of Christian philosophy as legitimate, but also boldly urges us to develop what he explicitly calls "Christian philosophy," which is not "an official philosophy of the Church, since the faith as such is not a philosophy"; rather it is "a Christian way of philosophizing, a philosophical speculation conceived [and practiced] in dynamic union with faith." (FeR §76) Philosophizing in faith, then, from an intrinsically Christian point of view, is not theology. Philosophy does respond to faith's own need for reflection, which is faith in search of understanding—*fides quaerens intellectum*; but that is theology. In a Christian way of philosophizing, faith enters the domain of reason "without ever demeaning the venture proper to reason" (FeR §78). And this is, the philosopher-Pope adds, "an undoubted boon for philosophy, which has thus glimpsed new vistas of further meanings which reason is summoned to penetrate" (FeR §101). In sum, he advises Christian philosophers "to illumine the range of human activity by the exercise of a reason which grows more penetrating and assured because of the support it receives from faith" (FeR §106).

Moreover, one aspect of Christian philosophy is the subjective dimension in which "faith purifies reason" (FeR §76). "Faith liberates reason from [the] presumption [of self-sufficiency]," adds John Paul, "the typical temptation of the philosopher." This is intellectual pride, which is an expression of "gnoseological concupiscence," or a "carnal mind," as St. Paul puts it (Col 2:18), the sinful inclination that sets us against God (FeR §§18-23). As a consequence, according to John Paul,

> The philosopher who learns humility [in faith] will also
> find courage to tackle questions which are difficult to
> resolve if the data of revelation are ignored—for example, the problem of evil and suffering, the personal nature of God and the question of the meaning of life or,
> more directly, the radical metaphysical question, "Why
> is there something rather than nothing?" (FeR §76).

This book is about all of the first three problems John Paul alludes to in this last citation—the problem of evil and suffering raises the fundamental question of human life's meaning, particularly the question of the meaning of suffering, and, in brief, of a suffering person's relationship with God—the blessed Trinity, Father, Son, and Holy Spirit—in whose redemptive action he "*reacts* to real suffering and real evil."[9] In respect of this last question, I shall consider the Catholic doctrine of redemptive suffering. On this view, adds Dupré, God "transforms the meaninglessness of suffering and evil into different patterns of meaning and goodness." How so? "In Christ God assumes all human suffering and takes upon himself the burden of compensating for all moral evil."[10] But there is more. In this doctrine, when those who suffer hopelessly unite their hopelessness with that of the crucified Son of God, he may "actually experience suffering itself as redemptive."[11] So, we will need to ask what sound theological sense can be given to the notion that by uniting our suffering with Christ's Passion we fulfill a role that God has given us, namely, to participate in the historical outworking of God's plan of salvation for the whole human race, which was accomplished in and through the finished work of Christ on the cross?

Sources of Evil and Suffering

There are several sources of evil and suffering: nature, or natural disasters; the vulnerabilities of our bodies, indeed, of our very selves; and, lastly, the evil committed by our fellow human beings.[12] We may call the former two "naturally occurring evil," or the evil suffered by men, such as, droughts, human illness, but also moral suffering, which is "pain of the soul," distinguished from physical suffering that is when "the body is hurting" (SD, §5); whereas the third instance may be simply called the evil that men do.[13] Regarding the evil that men do, this is the moral evil conceived and executed by human beings as a result of the misuse of their freedom. Says Davies, "With evil done we have a lack of goodness, and one without concomitant good explaining it or accounting for it" (Davies, 71). A reference to a concomitant good brings us to an account of the evil suffered. The evil or suffering in the former two is naturally explicable because their occurrence "is part of a system in which effects come about naturalistically and not as determined by us" (Davies, 68). The evil suffered is not caused by God as an end in itself;

rather, it is simply a by-product of the good system that God created. On this account of the evil suffered "there is always a concomitant good involved" (Davies, 70). He explains with some examples:

> God does not have to make people or viruses, but given that he has done so, human sickness is only to be expected. God does not have to make carnivores, but given that he has done so, they are going to have victims. God does not have to make plants, but given that he has done so, some are going to perish. At this point, however, an obvious question arises: is God causing evil insofar as he creates a world in which evil suffered can be found? (Davies, 68).

The answer to this question is that God has only caused what is good. Davies adds, "[The] evil suffered occurs only insofar as there is a concomitant good in the light of which it can be explained" (Davies, 69). Now, could God have created a world in which no evil could occur in it? (CCC, §310). Having created a system of nature such as ours God could not make a world "without material agents interacting and causing damage to each other" (Davies, 70). In this connection, we have the evils resulting from human free choices (Davies, 72).

Furthermore, we struggle to make sense in particular of the evil suffered by men, as I described it above, which is the evil that occurs through the natural environment. Says John Paul II, "Within each form of suffering endured by man, and at the same time as the basis of a whole world of suffering, there inevitably arises *the question*: Why? It is a question about the cause, the reason, and equally, about the purposes of suffering, and in brief, a question about its meaning" (SD, §9). In response to the suffering that we suffer personally but also with others, John Paul adds: "Human suffering evokes *compassion*; it also evokes *respect*, and in its own way *it intimidates*. For in suffering is contained the greatness of a specific mystery" (SD, §4).

The mystery is adumbrated in the experiences of personally suffering or of sharing in the sufferings of those one loves. Suffering, in other words, "in its subjective dimension, as a personal fact contained within man's concrete and unrepeatable interior," says the pope, "seems almost inexpressible and not transferable." Suffering is both subjective and passive, in the sense that it involves a submission such that I become the subject of suffering. But suffering is also marked by a "specific 'activity,'" that is, marked by the "multiple and subjectively differentiated 'activity' of pain, sadness, disappointment, discouragement or even despair, according to the intensity of the suffering subject" (SD, §7). This suffering degrades and alienates my very being because it appears to me to make no sense, to have no purpose, no justification, and to be of no use (SD, §27).[14] Yet "nothing else requires as much as does suffering," he adds, "*in its 'objective reality,'* to be dealt with, meditated upon, and conceived as an explicit problem; and that therefore basic questions be asked about it and the answers sought" (SD, §5).

In particular, in human suffering there is always the experience of some particular evil, whether in oneself or in others, as repugnant, and this experience raises two questions: (1) Is suffering intrinsically evil? And (2) What is evil?

I gave above several sources of evil and suffering. I distinguished "pain of the soul" from physical suffering that is when "the body is hurting." Consider now the many forms that these two kinds of suffering may take: chest pains from a heart attack, grief, loss or emptiness when a loved one dies, sorrow, desperation, sickness, righteous anger in the face of unjust oppression, deep repentance and guilt for one's sins, and so forth.[15] Can any of these kinds of suffering be shown to be good in some way? Pain has a biological function in serving as an alarm signal when something is going wrong with our body, warning us that we had better take appropriate action. As one author puts it, "It is known that approximately one out of every 400,000 babies born is fated to live a short life, due to a genetic disease called familial dysautonomia, a disease of feeling no pain. Such a child will cut himself, burn himself, fall down and break bones, without feeling any pain. Pain prevents us from doing any further damage.

As Harold B. Kushner says, pain seems to be the price we pay for being alive."[16] "Suffering also tempers the individual's character," says Emmanuel Levinas. As Nicholas Wolterstorff observes, "In the valley of suffering, despair and bitterness are brewed. But there also character is made. The valley of suffering is the vale of soul-making."[17]

The pain and suffering that accompany punishment, discipline and education also have a social function, because this contributes to the social order of society. Lastly, "no pain, no gain," is the common adage, and this seems right since there is no achievement in science, art, and architecture without paying the price of pain and suffering.

These and other instances of suffering involve accurate knowledge of human nature, our physical and moral makeup, which means that some suffering is, then, an appropriate reaction to some real state of affairs. Insofar as this is the case, then, despite the fact that human beings suffer whenever they encounter any kind of evil (SD, §7), the evil may be absorbed by an outweighing good and thus the suffering is not in itself evil; it is a positive reality, good in itself. As Germain Grisez has said: "Suffering generally also serves the important function of motivating people, as pain motivates animals to escape evil and/or struggle to overcome it…The evil of a heart attack is the destruction of part of the heart's tissue, not the pain in the chest which a conscious victim of heart attack experiences. (The pain causes heart attack victims to rest and seek help; if they felt no pain, death would be more likely.)"[18] One may thus say that the suffering is logically necessary for producing an outweighing good, which has absorbed the evil.[19] Some suffering can be meaningful as a means with an end in view, and thus in itself it is not evil. These points lead me to conclude that there is an important distinction to be made between suffering and evil.[20]

What, then, is evil? "Christianity proclaims the essential *good of existence* and the good of that which exists, acknowledges the goodness of the Creator and proclaims the good of creatures," according to John Paul II. Therefore evil is not a positive reality in its own ontological right. The pope embraces the Augustinian account of evil as a deprivation or distortion of a good that should have been but is not; in short, evil is an absence of the good. "We could say that a man suffers *because of a good* in which he does not share," he adds, "from which in a certain sense he is cut off, or of which he has deprived himself. He particularly suffers when he 'ought'—in the normal order of things—to have a share in this good, and does not have it" (SD, §7).

Free Will Defense

Whence, then, comes evil? Here, too, John Paul assumes the Augustinian free will defense: the moral evil conceived and executed by human beings is a result of the misuse of their freedom; they introduced evil into God's good creation. According to the pope,

> Sin was not only possible in the world in which man was created as a rational and free being, but it has been shown as an actual fact "from the very beginning." Sin is radical opposition to God. It is decidedly and absolutely not willed by God. However, he has permitted it by creating free beings, by creating the human race. He has permitted sin that is the consequence of the abuse of created freedom. This fact is known from revelation and experienced in its consequences. From it we can deduce that from the viewpoint of God's transcendent Wisdom, in the perspective of the finality of the entire creation [of human beings] it was more important that there should be freedom in the created world, even with the risk of its abuse, rather than to deprive the word of freedom by the radical exclusion of the possibility of sin.[21]

So the risk of evil is logically implied by the good of significantly free and rational creatures. According to the *Catechism*, "God is in no way, directly or indirectly, the cause of moral evil. He permits it, however, because he respects the freedom of his creatures and, mysteriously, knows how to derive good from it." Indeed, "In time we can discover that God in his almighty providence can bring a good from the consequences of an evil, even a moral evil, caused by his creatures." (CCC, §311-12) But it is not the generic good of human freedom that is the finality of their creation. If I understand John Paul II correctly, the outweighing good that significant freedom produces is the friendship of God. He says, "At the root, there is no mistaken or wicked decision by God, but rather his choice—and in a certain manner the risk he has undertaken—of creating us free, in order to have us as friends. Evil too has been born of liberty. But God does not give up, and he predestines us with his transcendent wisdom to be his children in Christ, directing all with strength and sweetness, so that the good may not be overcome by evil."[22]

The claim that sin results from the misuse of our free wills has often been used as a way of justifying the connection between suffering, punishment, and justice. According to Aidan Nichols, "From such sin there flows certain other aspects of human suffering, such as the physical pain inflicted by evil people, or the fear and anxiety which good people undergo when faced with the prospect of evil people. From moral evil there may also follow kinds of suffering which could be seen as divine punishment for sin."[23] In this view, we find a common response to suffering, which is to think of it as just punishment. Suffering is a punishment inflicted by God for humanity's moral evil. John Paul defends this suffering as a positive reality, or good in itself; it seems to be meaningful as a means with an end in view. As he says:

> The God of Revelation is the *Lawgiver and Judge* to a degree that no temporal authority can be. For the God of Revelation is first of all the Creator, from whom comes, together with existence, the essential good of creation. Therefore, the conscious and free violation of this good by man is not only a transgression of the law but at the same time and offense against the Creator, who is the first Lawgiver. Such a transgression has the character of sin…*Corresponding to the moral evil of sin is punishment*, which guarantees the moral order in the same transcendent sense in which this order is laid down by the will of the Creator and Supreme Lawgiver (SD, §10).

So God sometimes causes suffering as a just punishment for the moral evil of sin. But even more, suffering in this sense has meaning not only because the one who suffers does so justly as a punishment for sin, says the pope, "but first and foremost because it creates the possibility of rebuilding goodness in the subject who suffers." "This is an extremely important aspect of suffering," he adds, because "suffering must serve *for conversion*, that is, *for the rebuilding of goodness in the subject*, who can recognize the divine mercy in this call to repentance" (SD, §12).

In brief, suffering in this life is an educative punishment that should be regarded as good and justified because its purpose is to cultivate or strengthen goodness both in oneself and one's relationship with others and especially with God (SD, §12).[24] Such suffering may produce moral virtues, and hence character building is the outweighing good that absorbs some evil.

Significantly, John Paul II does not estimate the value of all suffering in terms of teleology. For instance, pain is meaningful and valuable because as an alarm signal it alerts us when something is wrong in our body; but the gratuitous pain that strikes the cancer patient and isolates him in his suffering already suggests the breakdown of this teleology as a complete explanation as to the meaning or purpose of the pain of suffering. In general, as John Paul says, "It is true that the universal experience teaches…the beneficial effects that pain has for so many as the source of maturity, wisdom, goodness, understanding, solidarity, so that one can speak of the fruitfulness of pain. But this observation leaves the basic problem unresolved."[25]

Furthermore, though it is undoubtedly true that the suffering allied with punishment is meaningful as a means with an end in view, all suffering cannot be justified in this way, says John Paul, because "*it is not true that all suffering is a consequence of a fault and has the nature of punishment*" (SD, §11). In other words, there is suffering without guilt, innocent suffering, because not all that suffer are being punished for moral evil. "Suffice to mention," he says, what I earlier called naturally occurring evil, or the evil suffered, that is, "natural disasters or calamities, and also all the forms of physical disability or of bodily or psychological diseases for which people are not blameworthy" (CoC, 269).

The Old Testament just man Job is decisive proof of this claim. As John Paul says, "Already in itself it is *sufficient argument* why the answer to the question about the meaning of suffering is not to be unreservedly linked to the moral order, based on justice alone." "While such an answer," he adds, "has a fundamental and transcendent reason and validity, at the same time it is seen to be not only unsatisfactory in cases similar to the suffering of the just man Job, but it even seems to trivialize and impoverish the *concept of justice* which we encounter in Revelation" (SD, §11). In short, there is more to suffering than guilt.

While it is true to say that the innocent also suffer, and hence they are not being punished for sin, it is also true and more important to understand that biblically there is only one class of persons, namely, sinners—all have sinned and come short of the glory of God (Rom 3:23). Saint Thomas Aquinas makes this important point in his commentary on Job.[26] He reminds us of the sinful character of human beings, even of those who innocently suffer and that suffering and tribulation of all sorts may help the sinner forward to the ultimate good of union with God. We read in the Epistle to the Hebrews: "For whom the Lord loves he chastens…Now no chastening seems to be joyful for the present, but painful; nevertheless, afterward it yields the peaceable fruit of righteousness to who have been trained by it" (12:6, 11).

Nevertheless, John Paul acknowledges that there are limits to estimating the value of all suffering as a just punishment for human sin. And so he wrestles with the traditional problem of evil that is usually presented as a dilemma for standard theism.[27] In his own words, the problem is thus: "How can evil and suffering be reconciled with that paternal solicitude, full of love, which Jesus Christ attributes to God in the Gospel? How are they to be reconciled with the transcendent wisdom and omnipotence of the Creator? And in a still more dialectical form—in the presence of all the experience of evil in the world, especially when confronted with the suffering of the innocent, can we say that God does not will evil? And if he wills it, how can we believe that 'God is love'?—all the more so since this love is omnipotent?"[28]

In other words, this problem is whether the propositions (1) "There is an omnipotent, omniscient, and perfectly good God" and (2) "There is evil in the world," are logically consistent in view of the claim that (3) "A perfectly good God would want to eliminate all of the evil that exists."

Other Theistic Response to the Problem

Besides the free will defense adumbrated above, John Paul sketches some other well-known theistic responses to the problem of evil and suffering. He accepts the validity of these arguments and thus he thinks that there are arguments available to show that evil's existence is not an insuperable intellectual obstacle to believing in a personal, infinite, and all-good God.[29] For instance, he accepts a version of the natural law theodicy—adumbrated above—in which evil is the by-product of the operation of a uniform natural order. God created a system of nature governed by natural laws for the sake of the goods that it alone can realize. Water is necessary for life but human lungs cannot absorb water without drowning. God foresees, but does not directly intend, that this and many other sorts of evil arise from the system of nature he has created. In other words, he permits yet does not intend and approve such evils. This divine permission, of course, is not to will evil directly and for its own sake. The evil in question is an unintended yet necessary consequence of a uniform natural order that produces certain kinds of good, for the victims of evil as well as for others. As Davies puts it, "Evil suffered . . . is caused by God *per accidens*."[30]

Something like this view is implied in the Pope's claim that God permits evil "in view of the overall good of the material cosmos."[31] This "indicates," he adds, "that God permits evil in the world for higher ends, but does not will it" (CoC, 273). So God is not the direct cause of evil, and he for a time tolerates evil only to bring about a greater good. Perhaps the most significant example of this is the crucified God: "From the greatest moral evil ever committed—the rejection and murder of God's only Son, caused by the sins of all men—God, by his grace that 'abounded all the more' [Rom 5:20], brought the greatest of goods: the glorification of Christ and our redemption. But for all that, evil never becomes a good" (CCC, §312).

Nonetheless, there are definite limits to the rational-abstract approach to the problem of evil and suffering, according to John Paul. Unlike many critics of theoretical theodicy, however, John Paul does not consider philosophical arguments and reflections on evil and suffering as irrelevant and immoral, but he does recognize their limitations. As he says:

> Why evil, why pain, why this human cross which seems co-essential to our nature, and yet, in so many cases, is absurd? They are questions which have always tormented the heart and mind of man and to which perhaps there can be given partial answers of a theoretical order, but which continue to crop up again in the reality of life, sometimes in a dramatic way, especially when it is the case of the suffering of the innocent, of children, and also of groups and entire peoples subjected to overbearing forces which seem to indicate in the world the triumph of evil. Which of us does not feel pierced to the heart in the presence of so many painful facts, so many crosses?[32]

The Limits of Theodicy

Two reasons, chiefly, stand out for the limitation of theoretical theodicy, as I understand John Paul's views.

(1) Let us suppose that there are valid defenses against the problem of evil showing that (a) the evils are logically necessary to the best of all possible worlds, or (b) that each evil is logically connected with some great enough good like a perfect balance of retributive justice, or (c) that the risk of evil is logically implied by the good of free creatures. These logically possible reasons are part of a general strategy for explaining why an omnipotent, omniscient, and perfectly good God would permit or allow evil to occur. This strategy expresses generic and global reasons, according to Marilyn McCord Adams. She explains, "generic in so far as some *general* reason is sought to cover all sorts of evils; global in so far as they seize upon some feature of the world as a whole."

Following Adams, I will also distinguish between two dimensions of God's goodness in relation to creation: God as "producer of global goods" and God's "goodness to or love of individual created persons."[33]

Now I think that John Paul II is concerned with the meaning of human life and, with it, human suffering in the context of an individual person's life. This concern leads him to think that fixing on generic and global goods as well as defending God's goodness *qua* producer of such goods is a mere abstract answer to the meaning of the individual person's suffering. Abstract insofar as, firstly, a theoretical global good theodicy discusses the evil of suffering at a general level rather than in terms of specificity and personal meaning, engaging the individual person who is suffering. As he sees it, an abstract general good theodicy does not clearly show God's providential care and love for human beings, leaving out of the picture how God, the transcendent good, relates himself to the evil of human suffering of individual persons.

Secondly, this theodicy is abstract insofar as these generic and global goods offer only a set of immanent, created goods rather than the infinite and uncreated goodness of God. And though John Paul II insists that God values human freedom even to the point of permitting evil to occur, his permission is justified only if it brings that person into union with God, which is humanity's highest good, in short, beatitude.

God created man with this desire in the human heart in order to draw us to himself, because God alone can fulfill this desire. "Man is created by God and for God"—in the words of the *Catechism of the Catholic Church* (§27). God has sought man out, a search that is biblically spoken of as the finding of a lost sheep (cf. Luke 15:1–7), and something that is attested in the Incarnation of the Son of God, Jesus Christ, the Redeemer of Man.

True God made true man, Jesus Christ reveals God's true nature to man but also shows him the path by which God may be reached. Christ is the answer to this desire in the heart of man, says John Paul II, "the only response fully capable of satisfying the desire of the human heart" (VS, §7). Jesus said, "I am the way, the truth, and the life. No one comes to the Father except through Me" (John 14:6). God calls us to his own beatitude, which is the perfect happiness of eternal life with him, promised us through the grace of Christ. "God put us in the world to know, to love, and to serve him, and so to come to paradise. Beatitude makes us 'partakers of the divine nature' (2 Pet 1:4) and of eternal life. With beatitude, man enters into the glory of Christ and into the joy of the Trinitarian life. Such beatitude surpasses the understanding and powers of man. It comes from an entirely free gift of God: Whence it is called supernatural, as is the grace that disposes man to enter into the divine joy."[34]

Friendship with God in his kingdom is sharing the life of the Holy Trinity. "For our fellowship is with the Father and with His Son Jesus Christ" (1 John 1:3). We are brought into this fellowship through the grace of Christ in conversion and baptism. And this fellowship is brought to its fulfillment, indeed, its eternal fullness in the Trinity's intimate revelation of the Father, Son, and Holy Spirit in the beatific vision. In short, this is our true happiness, our beatitude, which is the perfect happiness of eternal life with God, promised us through the grace of Christ. As Father Ashley puts it,

> Only by entering into the life of the ever-living Triune God, who is the source of all goodness, truth, and beauty, can every desire of created persons such as we are be satisfied. If we possess anything less than God, no matter how good it may be, our intelligences can always conceive of something better and our wills desire

that better thing. Only in God can we find that inexhaustible and infinite goodness that lacks nothing and thus can totally satisfy us as creatures endowed with intelligence and freedom. That cannot be said of any other things that humans desire, whether fame or fortune, health or pleasure, success or achievement, or the love of any creature.[35]

The implication that follows from believing that beatitude is the ultimate end of human existence, the chief end of man, and that the loss of this beatitude counts as definitive evil, is that a believer cannot be satisfied with exclusively immanent goods.[36]

(2) Let us suppose that a theoretical theodicy could show that the existence of God is compatible with the existence of evils of the amounts and kinds we find in the actual world, because they could be shown to be either not evils at all or evils necessarily built into the very idea of having a world in the first place. But even this approach has its limits. Aidan Nichols has made a decisive objection to it as a total response to the problem of evil, or so at least it seems to me. If this philosophical argument and others like it were, he says,

> an adequate and total vindication of the "justice of God," it would be exceedingly hard to find room for the theological concept of redemption, a concept which, however, lies at the heart of Christian faith. Thus Christian theodicists, aiming for total victory, swing their sabers and cut off their own heads...[in other words] if in theodicy we *could* clear up the problem of evil to our complete satisfaction, then there would be no need for salvation as presented in Christian revelation. God comes in His incarnate Son as the world's Redeemer, and by His Spirit as its Renewer, so as to repair the world's defects. But there would be no point in redemption if these defects could be shown to be either not defects at all or things built into the very idea of having a world in the first place.[37]

What, then, are some of the limits of theoretical theodicy? In classical Augustinian theodicy, evil is understood as the privation of good, but there also needs to be an account of the "strange potency of evil."

That in the first place. In the second place, we must avoid flattening out the difference between humanity as God created it and humanity as it exists in a fallen state. Otherwise, the problem arises that we lose sight of the *contingency* of evil.

This problem is clearly identified by James Orr early in the twentieth century. He wrote, "If sin lies in the constitution of things by creation—if it is a necessary outcome of the condition in which God made man, and of the nature He has given him—how can the creature be asked to assume responsibility—at least serious responsibility for it?"[38] So, we need to give an account of the fall of man, in short, of original sin. Nichols adds two other limitations. "Third, there is the apparent escape of nature from the rational control of Providence as evidenced in say, the suffering of the innocent in natural disasters." In the fourth place, "the absence of sufficient meaning, our inability to make anything like complete sense of the world."[39]

The Idea of Salvation

These limitations raise certain questions that can be answered in the Christian idea of salvation. Nichols explains:

> If the [Second Person of the Blessed Trinity] entered our world as the Redeemer, he must, it seems, do four things. He must conquer and neutralize the potency of evil in its fundamental ground. He must give finite spirits a new supernatural principle of action to replace that given them by original sin. He must provide for the harmonization of nature with human happiness. He must overcome the ambiguity, or absence of sufficient meaning in human life, as we know it. But if there is to be such a redemptive action by God, then there must be some way in which we can apprehend his involvement with the world.[40]

We will return to these points in the next chapter. For now, I should note that John Paul agrees with Nichols about the limits of theoretical theodicy, and he puts it in his own words as follows:

> In God's eternal plan, and in His providential action

in human history, every evil, and in particular moral evil—sin—is subjected to the good of the redemption and salvation precisely through the cross and resurrection of Christ. It can be said that in Him God draws forth good from evil. He does it in a certain sense from the very evil of sin, which was the cause of the suffering of the Immaculate Lamb and of His terrible death on the cross as a victim for the sins of the world. The Church's liturgy does not hesitate even to speak, in this regard, of the 'happy fault' (*felix culpa*; cf. *Exsultet* of the Easter Vigil Liturgy). Thus a definitive answer cannot be given to the question about the reconciliation of evil and suffering with the truth of divine providence, without reference to Christ (CoC, 273-74).

The question arises here as to whether the pope thinks that the unthinkably great good of the incarnation and redemption outweighs and justifies all the evil in the world. This passage clearly suggests that all evil in the world is absorbed by the single good of redemption and salvation. But what remains unclear is whether in his account of redemptive suffering John Paul II thinks that this good ultimately overcomes or defeats rather than justifies evil, in the sense that there is a logically necessary connection between the evils that occur and the good justifying God's permitting them.

Yet what is abundantly clear is John Paul's insistence that the cross of Christ redeems both sin and suffering. "In the cross of Christ not only is the Redemption accomplished through suffering, *but also human suffering itself has been redeemed...* In bringing about the Redemption through suffering, Christ *has* also *raised human suffering to the level of Redemption.*"[41] "Thus each man," he adds, "in his suffering can also become a sharer in the redemptive suffering of Christ" (SD, §19).

The cross does not only alter our perspective about suffering. Most important, by Christ's passion, John Paul says, all suffering is objectively and in principle changed, assumed in "a completely new dimension and a new order" (SD, §18). This means, as I understand it, that "suffering loses its prima facie negative character for the victim by being given a transcendent, positive meaning."[42] Says John Paul, "One can say that with the passion of Christ all human suffering has found itself in a new situation" (SD, §19). And as John Paul also says, "Christ's cross—the passion—throws a completely new light on this problem [of evil] by conferring another meaning on human suffering in general."[43]

In other words, the right kind of connection is apparently made here between an individual's suffering and the single good of incarnation and redemption: not only is God's providential care and love for human beings definitively and unsurpassably manifested in his conquering or overcoming evil through the saving work of Christ crucified, but also suffering can be redemptive for myself and for others, provided I unite it with the sufferings of Christ. In short, I must take up my cross and follow the Lord (Mark 8:34).

Furthermore, God is not an impersonal absolute that remains outside of human history, cold and distant from human suffering, according to John Paul II. "He is Emmanuel, God-with-us, a God who shares man's lot and participates in his destiny." "God is not someone who remains only outside the world," the pope adds, "content to be in Himself all-knowing and omnipotent. *His wisdom and omnipotence are placed, by free choice, at the service of creation.* If suffering is present in the history of humanity, one understands why His omnipotence was manifested *in the omnipotence of humiliation on the Cross.* The scandal of the Cross remains the key to the interpretation of the great mystery of suffering, which is so much a part of the history of mankind... Christ *is proof of God's solidarity with man in his suffering.*"[44] Thus, in the mystery of redemptive suffering God himself participates in human suffering.

As a personalist, John Paul understands God's response to human suffering to be a personal response of love. Indeed, the true answer to the question of why we suffer must be found in the revelation of divine love, which is the ultimate meaning-giving source of everything that exists, including suffering. "This answer has been given by God to man in the cross of Jesus Christ," according to John Paul (SD, §13).

As the supreme mystery of divine love, Christ is the greatest possible answer to the question about suffering and the meaning of suffering. He is the answer, says the Pope, "not only by His teaching, that is, by the Good News, but most of all by His own suffering, which is integrated with this teaching of the Good News in an organic and indissoluble way." "And this is," adds John Paul II, "*the final,* definitive word of this *teaching*: 'the word of the cross,' as St. Paul one day will say" (SD, §18).

The cross is, then, the answer to the problem of evil, but this answer is not a theoretical one that refutes all objections. "Love is," according to the pope, "the richest source of the meaning of suffering, which always remains a mystery: we are conscious of the insufficiency and inadequacy of our explanations. Christ causes us to enter into the mystery and to discover the 'why' of suffering, as far as we are capable of grasping the sublimity of divine love" (SD, §13).

So I now intend to look, in Chapter 3, first at the whole matter of Christ's cross as God's redemptive response to real suffering and real evil; then at how God in Christ is present in human suffering; and finally, in Chapter 4, at the meaning of suffering in the light of Christ's passion, death, and resurrection.

Notes

1. Dupré, "Philosophy and the Mystery of Evil," 60.

2. Étienne Gilson, *The Philosopher and Theology*, 228-29.

3. John Paul's conception of Christian philosophy may be traced backed to Gilson's influence on his thought. Gilson himself claims to owe his conception of Christian philosophy to the "epoch-making document" of Pope Leo XIII, the 1879 Encyclical Letter *Aeterni Patris*. The late Catholic intellectual Michael Novak has argued that Karol Wojtyla (aka John Paul II) "was much taken with the argument on Christian philosophy launched by Etienne Gilson" ("The Christian Philosophy of John Paul II," in *On Cultivating Liberty*, 243-56).

4. John Paul II, *Salvifici Doloris*, Apostolic Letter, 11 February 1984. Neo-Calvinist philosopher Alvin Plantinga praises this papal document highly: "*Salvifici Doloris* [is] surely one of the finest documents (outside the Bible) ever written on this topic, and surely required reading for anyone interested in the so-called problem of evil, or the problems that suffering can pose for the Christian spiritual life or, more generally, the place of suffering in the life of the Christian." Nicolas Wolterstorff, Richard J. Bernstein, and Alvin Plantinga, review of *Fides et Ratio, Books and Culture*, July/August 1999:32. In the third volume of his trilogy on the notion of warrant entitled *Warranted Christian Belief*, Plantinga repeats his judgment that *Salvifici Doloris* is "a profound meditation on suffering and a powerful effort to discern its meaning from a Christian perspective"; indeed, he calls it a "seminal work" in the "larger project of Christian scholarship, of discerning the ways in which Christian belief illuminates many of the important areas of human concern" (§38 and §46, at 488 and 493, respectively).

5. Del Kiernan-Lewis, *Learning to Philosophize*, 61-62.

6. Dupré, "Philosophy and the Mystery of Evil," 54.

7. Ibid., 59. The quote within quotes is from Marilyn McCord Adams, "Problems of Evil: More Advice to Christian Philosophers," 129.

8. Maritain, *The Peasant of the Garonne*, 142.

9. Dupré, "Philosophy and the Mystery of Evil," 58.

10. Ibid., 60.

11. Ibid.

12. Os Guinness, *Unspeakable*, 19-34.

13. Davies, *Thomas Aquinas on God and Evil*, 68, 71.

14. On this aspect of suffering, see Y.A. Kang, "Levinas on Suffering and Solidarity," 482-504; Stan van Hooft, "The Meaning of Suffering," 13-19; and Emmanuel Levinas, "Useless Suffering," in *The Provocation of Levinas: Rethinking Other*, 156-67.

15. Grisez, *The Way of the Lord Jesus*, vol. 2, 31-32.

16. Kang, "Levinas on Suffering and Solidarity," 487.

17. Wolterstorff, *Lament for a Son*, 97.

18. Grisez, *The Way of the Lord Jesus*, vol. 2, 32. See also John Saward, *Christ Is the Answer*, especially 85-89. I owe much both to Grisez's and Saward's short reflections on human suffering. Also helpful in this regard is Avery Dulles, S.J., *The Splendor of Faith*, 89-93.

19. On the notion of absorbed evils, see J. L. Mackie, *The Miracle of Theism*, 154.

20. Guinness, *Unspeakable*, 24.

21. *CoC*, 260. He places great value on significant freedom: "Full of paternal solicitude, God's authority implies full respect for freedom in regard to rational and free beings. In the created world, this freedom is an expression of the image and likeness to the divine Being itself, to divine freedom itself. Respect for created freedom is so essential that God in his Providence even permits human sin (and that of the angels). Pre-eminent among all but always limited and imperfect, the rational creature can make evil use of freedom, and can use it against God, the Creator...In the case of moral evil, however, that is, of sin and guilt in their different forms and consequences also in the physical order, this evil decisively and absolutely is not willed by God. Moral evil is radically contrary to God's will. If in human history this evil is present and at times overwhelming, if in a certain sense it has its own history, it is only permitted by divine Providence because God wills that there should be freedom in the created world. The existence of created freedom (and therefore the existence of man, and the existence of pure spirits such as the angels...), is indispensable for that fullness of creation which corresponds to God's eternal plan...By reason of that fullness of good which God wills to be realized in creation, the existence of free beings is for Him a more important and fundamental value than the fact that those beings may abuse their freedom against the Creator, and that freedom can therefore lead to moral evil" (259, 271).

22. Ibid., 316-17. On the same point, the Holy Father writes earlier in the same work:

"By God's Providence, however, if on the one hand he has permitted sin, on the other, with the loving solicitude of a father, he has foreseen from eternity the way of reparation, of redemption, of justification and of salvation through love. Freedom is ordained to love. Without freedom there cannot be love. In the conflict between good and evil, between sin and redemption, love has the last word" (260).

23. Nichols, *The Shape of Catholic Theology*, 68.

24. Grisez correctly qualifies this point that suffering is an educative punishment. He says, "In the next life, of course, those who persisted in evil will experience their own wretchedness, and their punishment no longer will be educative" (Living a Christian Life, 32).

25. John Paul II, General Audience (30 March 1983), published in *L'Obsservatore Romano*, 5 April 1983: 4.

26. On this, see Eleonore Stump, "Aquinas on the Sufferings of Job," in *The Evidential Argument from Evil*, ed. Daniel Howard-Snyder, 49-68. See also Helm, *The Last Things: Death, Judgment, Heaven, and Hell*, 72.

27. By standard theism I am referring to what William L. Rowe has called "any view which holds that there exists an omnipotent, omniscient, omnigood being who created the world." Rowe also distinguishes within standard theism two views: restricted theism and expanded theism. "Expanded theism is the view that [God] exists, conjoined with certain other significant religious claims, claims about sin, redemption, a future life, a last judgment, and the like. (Orthodox Christian theism is a version of expanded theism). Restricted theism is the view that God exists, unaccompanied by other, independent religious claims" ("Evil and the Theistic Hypothesis: A Response to Wykstra," in The Problem of Evil, 160).

28. *CoC*, 269. The pope raises a somewhat different but related question in *Crossing the Threshold of Hope*, pp. 60-61: "We cannot forget that in every century, at the hour of truth, even Christians have asked themselves a tormenting question: How to continue to trust in a God who is supposed to be a merciful Father, in a God who—as the New Testament reveals—is meant to be Love itself, when suffering, injustice, sickness, and death seem to dominate the larger history of the world as well as our smaller daily lives?"

29. Ibid., 271-72: "Undoubtedly it is a great light we receive from reason and revelation in regard to the mystery of divine Providence which, while not willing the evil, tolerates it in view of a greater good." Yet, John Paul adds clearly, "However, the definitive light can come to us only from the victorious cross of Christ."

30. Davies, *Thomas Aquinas on God and Evil*, 70.

31. *CoC*, 270-71: "Sacred Scripture assures us that: 'against wisdom evil does not prevail' (Wisdom 7:30). This strengthens our conviction that in the Creator's providential plan in regard to the world, in the last analysis evil is subordinated to good. Moreover, in the context of the integral truth about divine Providence, one is helped to better understand the two statements: 'God does not will evil as such' and 'God permits evil.' In regard to the first it is opportune to recall the words of the Book of Wisdom: 'God did not make death, and He does not delight in the death of the living. For He created all things that they may exist' (Wisdom

1:13-14). As regards the permission of evil in the physical order, e.g., the fact that material beings (among them also the human body) are corruptible and undergo death, it must be said that this belongs to the very structure of the being of these creatures. In the present state of the material world, it would be difficult to think of the unlimited existence of every individual corporeal being. We can therefore understand that, if 'God did not make death,' as the Book of Wisdom states, He nonetheless permitted it in view of the overall good of the material cosmos."

32. L'Obsservatore Romano, 5 April 1983: 4.

33. Marilyn McCord Adams, "Horrendous Evils and the Goodness of God," in *The Problem of Evil*, 213. See also her book-length treatment, *Horrendous Evils and the Goodness of God*, particularly 29-30.

34. *CCC*, §§27, 1718–19, and for this quote at 1721–22.

35. Ashley, *Living the Truth in Love*, 95.

36. Dupré, "Philosophy and the Mystery of Evil," 59.

37. Nichols, *The Shape of Catholic Theology*, 70-72.

38. *God's Image in Man and Its Defacement in the Light of Modern Denials*, 1903-1904 Stone Lectures, Princeton Theological Seminary, 206-7.

39. Nichols, *The Shape of Catholic Theology*, 72.

40. Ibid., 72-73.

41. I return in the next chapter to the all-important question, in what sense is suffering redeemed? It seems clear to say, in the light of Christian soteriology, that our sins have been redeemed by the passion and death of Christ, but John Paul's frequent assertion in *SD* that "human suffering itself has been redeemed" (§19) is not easily understood.

42. Stan van Hooft, "The Meanings of Suffering," 15.

43. *CoC*, vol. II, 453-54: "The redemption carried out by Christ at the price of his passion and death on the cross is a decisive event in human history, not only because it fulfills the supreme divine plan of justice and mercy, but also because it gave new meaning to the problem of suffering. No problem has weighed more heavily on the human family, especially in its relationship with God. We know that the value of human existence is conditioned by the solution of the problem of suffering. To a certain extent it coincides with the problem of evil, whose presence in the world is so difficult to accept…Thanks to Christ, the meaning of suffering changes radically. It no longer suffices to see in it a punishment for sin. One must discern in it the redemptive, salvific power of love. The evil of suffering, in the mystery of Christ's redemption, is overcome and in every case transformed."

44. John Paul II, *Crossing the Threshold of Hope*, 62-63.

CHAPTER 3

The Crucified God

Jesus Christ: Evil and Suffering
Defeated by Divine Love

Fundamentally, the reason that Christ is the unique mediator of salvation, and the savior, is that Christ alone is God. Because he is God made human, Jesus' human actions and sufferings have an infinite dignity of a mysterious kind. There is no human sin that is so great that God cannot make reparation for it in his human actions and sufferings.[1]

Christian soteriology, which is the theology of salvation dealing with God's atoning work in Christ, is multifaceted, involving sacrifice, substitution, satisfaction, but particularly significant for our discussion in this book is the divine victory over sin and the evils of human suffering and death.[2]

Salvation addresses the various aspects of sin: sin is like an illness, it's about moral guilt, an enslaving force that has a stranglehold on us, and a conflict between two ways of life[3]—"The way of Christ 'leads to life'; a contrary way 'leads to destruction'" (CCC §1696). This conflict is also expressed in the New Testament as the conflict between "death and life (Rom 6:3-8), darkness and light (John 1:5; 1 Pet 2:9), sin and grace (Rom 5:20-6:1), lostness and 'being found' (note the three parables of Luke 15)."[4]

Furthermore, the evils of suffering pertain not only to temporal suffering. Rather, the definitive evil and therefore the definitive suffering that humanity can know is eternal separation from God, who is the supreme good. Hence alienation from God is the heart of sin. God's atoning work in Christ deals with that alienation. As the *Catechism of the Catholic Church* states: "God put us in the world to know, to love, and to serve him, and so to come to paradise. Beatitude makes us 'partakers of the divine nature' and of eternal life. With beatitude, man enters into the glory of Christ and into the joy of Trinitarian life." Beatitude is, the *Catechism* adds, "not found…in any creature, but in God alone, the source of every good and of all love" (CCC §1721).

The loss of beatitude, rejection by God, damnation and the loss of eternal life is the fundamental and definitive meaning of suffering that is the result of alienation from God because of unrepentant sin (ibid., §1861). According to John Paul II, the love of the Father is manifested in the gift of his only-begotten Son, whose salvific work is communicated through the Holy Spirit. In his salvific mission, Christ strikes at the very roots of evil, which are sin and death, freeing humanity from the loss of eternal life and, with it, our suffering in its fundamental and definitive meaning. "The mission of the only-begotten Son consists in *conquering sin and death*. He conquers sin by His obedience unto death," says the pope, "and He overcomes death by His resurrection" (SD §14).

In this connection, we need to say something briefly about the relation of justice and mercy in Christian soteriology.[5] To understand properly the reality of God's merciful pardon and how it is that mercy triumphs over judgment (Jas 2:13), we cannot minimize the wrath of God. God's wrath is His response to the sins of men (Eph 2:4)—His holy displeasure against their sin (NGM §32) that entails the breaking of communion with Him (MV §2)—as the expression of His fundamental justice, righteousness, and holiness.

Given his holiness, then, God's response to sin and evil is resistance, revulsion, his holy displeasure to all that opposes him, and this response the Sacred Scriptures call—says Kasper rightly—"the wrath of God" (Eph 2:3).[6] He adds: "But God's wrath does not mean an emotionally surging rage or an angry intervention, but rather [his] resistance to sin and injustice. Wrath is, so to speak, the active and dynamic expression of his holy essence.

For this reason, the message of judgment cannot be expunged from the message of the Old or New Testament or be harmlessly interpreted away. God's holiness conforms to his justice." In sum, muting or suppressing God's wrath, judgment, and holiness, in short, the justice of God, turns "the message of God's mercy," Kasper concludes, into "a message of cheap grace," and hence we will not know the greatness of mercy. As Pope Francis has recently described that mercy:

> "But without forgetting that we were estranged from Him because of original sin, which separated us from our Father: our filial relationship was profoundly wounded. Therefore, God sent his Son to rescue us at the price of His blood. And if there is a rescue, it is because there is a slavery. We were children, but we became slaves, following the voice of the Evil One. No one else rescues us from that essential slavery except Jesus, who assumed our flesh from the Virgin Mary and died on the cross to free us from the slavery of sin and to restore us to our lost filial condition."[7]

When we reflect on mercy the question naturally arises about the relationship of mercy to justice. God is not merciful *at the expense of* his justice. Mercy does not exclude His justice, nor is it opposed to it (MV §21). How could it? "God's justice is his mercy given to everyone [oppressed by slavery to sin and its consequences] as a grace that flows from the death and resurrection of Jesus Christ (ibid.)."

God's justice entails His taking sin seriously, indeed, "of all the injustice we have committed before God" (NGM §58), by virtue of taking away and atoning for our guilt in history. In the reality of the atoning work of Jesus Christ there is a turning from real wrath to real grace.

Pope Francis explains, "Thus the Cross of Christ is God's judgment on all of us and on the whole world (MV §21)." Here Francis echoes John Paul II who teaches that God has shown us his justice and mercy "in the cross of Christ, on which the Son, consubstantial with the Father, *renders full justice to God.*" His death on the cross, he adds, "is also *a radical revelation of mercy*, or rather of *the love* that goes against what constitutes the very root of evil in the history of man: against sin and death" (DM §8, emphasis added).

Jesus Christ's finished work is the full and sufficient cause of our salvation. He has undergone the cross because of our sins, redeeming us from them, healing us from the deep wound of original sin and its effects (NGM, 42-43; MV §22), and reconciling us to the Father in the power of the Spirit (2 Cor 5:19). His atoning work "constitutes even a 'superabundance' of justice, for the sins of man are 'compensated for' by the sacrifice of the man-God" (DM §7).

The reference to "superabundance" of justice is an allusion to its perfection, its excess: past, present, and future sins are fully satisfied by Christ's death on the cross. Further, it refers to the "excessive" character of God's reconciling act in that God gives himself in the self-sacrificial love of Jesus' death for his enemies. "When we were God's enemies we were reconciled to him through the death of his Son" (Rom 5:10).

The interrelationship between justice and mercy (NGM, 77), of the wrathful and forgiving God, in the light of the cross, which is the manifestation of the fullness of God's love, is key to understanding "God's way of reaching out to the sinner, offering him a new chance to look at himself, convert, and believe" (MV §21). Francis adds: "Salvation comes ... through faith in Jesus Christ, who in his death and resurrection brings salvation together with a mercy that justifies" (ibid.).

Justice and Mercy as Aspects of God's Love

God's love is inseparably connected with his holiness and his justice, and hence God therefore must manifest his wrath when confronted with sin and evil. Yes, of course the gospel is an expression of the love of God, indeed, the supreme example: "This is how God showed his love among us: He sent his one and only Son into the world that we might live through him. This is love: not that we loved God, but that he loved us and sent his Son as an atoning sacrifice for our sins" (1 John 4:9-10). Yet God's love is never expressed at the expense of any other attribute of his character, such as his holiness and wrath, the latter being God's holy reaction to evil and sin.

> "It would be offensive to speak of God's wrath if we did not also know of His holiness and love. But, just as man must repent his sins to enter into God's grace, so the believer must approach the mystery of God's anger if he will rightly approach God's love. To wish to reduce the mystery of divine wrath to a mythical expression of human experience is to mistake the seriousness of sin and to forget the tragic side of God's love. There is a fundamental incompatibility between holiness and sin."[8]

In sum, the wrath of God is the real and effective opposition to sin of the all-holy God, that is, "the revelation of the *absolute distance* and the radical and clear antithesis between God and man's sin."[9] In the words of the then Joseph Ratzinger on the matter of God's wrath:

> From this [the reality of sin] one can understand what the 'wrath of God' and the anger of the Lord are all about: necessary expressions of his love that is always identical with the truth. A Jesus who is in agreement with everybody and anybody, a Jesus without his holy wrath, without the toughness of the truth and of true love, is not the true Jesus as Scripture shows him but a miserable caricature. A presentation of the "gospel" in which the seriousness of God's wrath no longer exists has nothing to do with the biblical gospel. . . . A Jesus who approves of everything is a Jesus without the cross, because the tribulation of the cross would not then be needed to bring men and women salvation.[10]

In short, God cannot simply overlook sins; his justice must be satisfied in some way. The cross is a satisfaction. "[It] constitutes even a 'superabundance' of justice," says John Paul, "for the sins of man are 'compensated for' by the sacrifice of the God-man." The reference to the "superabundance" of justice is an allusion to its perfection, its excess: past, present and future sins are fully satisfied by Christ's death on the cross.

But it means more than this allusion. Chiefly, I think, it refers to the "excessive" character of God's reconciling act in the death of Christ. This saving act is "excessive" in that God gives himself in the self-sacrificial love of Jesus' death on the cross *for his enemies*. The cross is an act of merciful justice, and the mercy is a just mercy. "When we were God's enemies we were reconciled to him through the death of his Son" (Rom 5:10).

Nevertheless, it is not an angry and remote God that sinners need to placate before he can love and forgive; the gospel is an expression of the love (mercy) of God, prior to any merit on our part. As Joseph Ratzinger puts it in his classic 1968 study, *Introduction to Christianity*, "It is not man who goes to God with a compensatory gift, but God who comes to man, in order to give to him. He restores disturbed right on the initiative of his own power to love, by making unjust man just again, the dead living again, through his own creative mercy. His righteousness is grace; it is active righteousness, which sets crooked man right, that is, bends him straight, makes him correct. . . . God does not wait until the guilty come to be reconciled; he goes to meet them and reconciles them. Here we can see the true direction of the Incarnation, of the Cross."[11]

This point is so important that it is worth repeating.[12] In the words of Presbyterian theologian, John Murray, "It is one thing to say that the wrathful God is made loving. *That would be entirely false.* It is another thing to say the wrathful God is loving. That is profoundly true. But it is also true that the wrath by which he is wrathful is propitiated through the cross. This propitiation is the fruit of divine love that provided it. . . . The propitiation is the ground upon which the divine love operates and the channel through which it flows in achieving its end."[13]

So both justice and mercy have their origin in God's holy love, but how so? To deal with this issue of the relation of mercy and justice, then, we need to turn to atonement because it is in the cross of Christ that God's justice, mercy, and love are *simultaneously* revealed.[14] These two, says John Paul, spring completely from love: "from the love of the Father and of the Son, and completely bears fruit in love" (DM §7).

Pope Francis explains that "these [justice and mercy] are not two contradictory realities, but two dimensions of a single reality that unfolds progressively until it culminates in the fullness of love" (MV §20). God's love is the single reality that unfolds dynamically throughout salvation history in the dimensions of justice and mercy with these two harmoniously coming together supremely in the cross.

In sum, the cross takes our sins away because it is the act of God's gracious judgment on Christ for our benefit: "For our sake he made him to be sin who knew no sin, so that in him we might become the righteousness of God" (2 Cor 5:21). The basis of this act is divine love: "In this is love, not that we loved God but that he loved us and sent his Son as an atoning sacrifice for our sins" (1 John 4:10). "For God so loved the world that he gave his one and only Son, that whoever believes in him shall not perish but have eternal life" (John 3:16). "But God demonstrates his own love for us in this: While we were still sinners, Christ died for us" (Rom 5:8). "But because of his great love for us, God, who is rich in mercy, made us alive with Christ even when we were dead in transgressions—it is by grace you have been saved" (Eph 2:4-5).

This saving act arises at once from the will of the Son and of the Father: "By his obedience unto death, Jesus accomplished the substitution of the suffering Servant, who 'makes himself an *offering for sin*', when 'he bore the sin of many', and who 'shall make many to be accounted righteous', for 'he shall bear their iniquities.' Jesus atoned for our faults and made satisfaction for our sins to the Father" (CCC §615). St. Paul writes, "Since we have now been justified by his blood, how much more shall we be saved from God's wrath through him. For if, when we were God's enemies, we were reconciled to him through the death of his Son, how much more, having been reconciled, shall we be saved through his life" (Rom 5:9-10).

The Response Factor

The way the believer receives the grace of Christ's atoning work, his gift of infinite mercy, is by faith (Rom 3:21-25; Eph 2:8-9). Thus, Pope Francis identifies the need "to recognize our emptiness, our wretchedness" (NGM, 43), "of our need for forgiveness and mercy," in short, to confess "our miseries, our sins" in order to obtain mercy by faith in Jesus Christ (ibid., 32). Sin is not only a stain upon our soul, but it is also "a wound," Francis teaches, that "needs to be treated, healed" (ibid., 26). Approaching the Lord of mercy with confidence requires, adds Francis, "a shattered heart," meaning thereby, having "consciousness of our sins, of the evil we have done, of our wretchedness, and of our need for forgiveness and mercy" (ibid., 32).

Of course even this recognition of oneself as a sinner and the corresponding act of repentance stems from an act of grace that is the Lord's gift to us. Furthermore, we have the promise, Pope Francis tirelessly emphasizes, that "if we confess our sins he is faithful and just to forgive us our sins and to cleanse us from all unrighteousness" (1 John 1:9).

Of course, without repentance and God's forgiveness, the impenitent sinner calls God a liar, deceives himself, and the truth is not in him. In consequence, the state of the impenitent sinner "causes exclusion from Christ's kingdom and the eternal death of hell" (CCC §1861). Still, Christians pray for the perfection of divine love in our life so that we may stand by God's grace in the Day of Judgment without fear. "There is no fear in love. But perfect love drives out fear, because fear has to do with punishment. The one who fears is not made perfect in love" (1 John 4:17-18). So, mercy triumphs over judgment. Mercy is the face of God's love toward sinners, and that divine love is fully realized in the cross of Calvary.

Redemptive Sufficiency of Christ's Atoning Work

Because of the redemptive sufficiency of Christ's salvific work in striking evil right at its roots, evil and definitive eschatological suffering is totally vanquished. "For God so loved the world that He gave His only-begotten Son, that whoever believes in Him should not perish but have eternal life" (John 3:16). Yet there is still more: "*evil and suffering in their temporal and historical dimension*" (SD §15), says John Paul, are also struck at their roots.

What this means is that in the death and resurrection of Jesus Christ there is also victory over sin and death in this earthly life, here and now. Nonetheless, though the dominion of sin and death are defeated in Jesus Christ, says John Paul II, "His cross and resurrection does not abolish temporal suffering from human life, nor free from suffering the whole historical dimension of human existence" (SD §15).

So much is this the case, one might add, that there still remains about as much reason as ever to wonder whether perhaps Christ was victorious over the dominion of sin and death in his cross and resurrection. I have no doubt of the Spirit's power to heal now, this side of eternity.[15] Yet we must also put front and center in our dealing with redemptive suffering Jesus' call that we should take up our cross and follow him (Matt 16:24). This holds particularly in cases where our suffering is like a thorn in the flesh. St. Paul speaks to this:

> "Concerning this thing I pleaded with the Lord three times that it might depart from me. And He said to me, 'My grace is sufficient for you, for My strength is made perfect in weakness.' Therefore, most gladly I will rather boast in my infirmities, that the power of Christ may rest upon me. Therefore, I take pleasure in infirmities, in reproaches, in needs, in persecutions, in

distresses, for Christ's sake. For when I am weak, then I am strong" (2 Cor 12: 8-10).

Still, there's an obvious question: why, if the dominion of sin and death has been defeated, isn't evil and suffering in their temporal and historical dimension abolished? In other words, why the divine permission for evil and suffering?

Benedict Ashley makes the same point even clearer: "Even if the promise [in Romans 8:18-24] that God in his justice will more than compensate in our future life for every suffering in the present and will see to it that our efforts to help others will not have been in vain, the subjective problem remains: Why has an all-powerful God permitted us to suffer so much *here and now*? Why has he not eliminated the suffering and simply given us happiness that after all is ultimately his gift to give?"[16] John Paul faces this vexing question head-on, as we shall see below.

For now, it suffices to understand that Christ's saving work defeats the dominion of sin and, with it, its presence and power in human life that took root in human nature with original sin. We need to consider the doctrine of original sin, even if only briefly, in order to answer the question, in what sense is our suffering redeemed? What, then, is original sin? It is necessary to consider this question in order to show how Jesus Christ, here and now, not only conquers and neutralizes the dominion of evil but also gives man "a new supernatural principle of action to replace that given them by original sin."[17] Because of original sin and personal sin, then, "The human heart is heavy and hardened. God must give man a new heart. Conversion is first of all a work of the grace of God who makes our hearts return to him" (CCC §1432). I said in Chapter 2 that I would address this aspect of the Christian view of salvation, and I do so now.

Original Sin

Following the teaching of the Catholic Church, the orthodox Christian doctrine of original sin has the following four points, which John Paul II develops in Volume II of his *Catechesis on the Creed: Jesus, Son and Savior*. First, original sin is *universal sinfulness*, consisting of attitudes, tendencies, and an inclination to sin, to evil, that the Council of Trent called "concupiscence," and which are contrary to God's will, at odds with his holiness, and present in all persons, in all areas of their lives. Second, original sin is *natural sinfulness*: it belongs to human nature in a real sense, and is present from birth; we are born with a fallen human nature. Third, original sin is *inherited sinfulness*: this fallen human nature is inherited which results in human beings that are born in a state or condition of hereditary moral weakness and alienation or estrangement from God, now having lost the grace of original holiness and righteousness. And fourth, original sin is *Adamic sinfulness*: it stems from Adam, who committed the first sin and whose disobedience toward God gave original sin a historical beginning, and which has left its consequence in every descendant of Adam, so that the sinful situation of humanity is connected with the fault of Adam, the first man and progenitor of the race.[18]

We do not yet have original sin fully in view, however. Original sin underscores, firstly, the Church's insistence on the *contingency* of evil. As Father Nichols rightly states: "Sin must have entered human life at some historical moment...For unless evil marred the creation of humanity contingently (i.e., historically), it could only have done so essentially (i.e., by God's own creative act), which is unthinkable. In claiming Adam (with Eve) as historical figures, the Church is confirmed by the New Testament, especially by Paul's appeal to Adam's fall as the act which Christ's redemptive act inverted. Revelation presents both as historical events with metahistorical meaning."[19]

Secondly, the consequence of original sin is death, so that "we die not because we commit individual sins of our own volition; rather we sin, and *inevitably*, we die, and *inevitably*, as a result of Adam's sin."[20] The upshot of the doctrine of original sin, says the pope, is that it helps us to "understand the mysterious and distressing aspects of evil which [we] daily experience." Otherwise we "end up by wavering between a hasty and unjustified optimism and a radical pessimism bereft of hope." (CoC, II, 42).

John Henry Cardinal Newman was also persuaded that the doctrine of original sin was necessary to explain evil in our world in light of faith in God's goodness and omnipotence: "either there is no Creator, or this living society of men is in a true sense discarded from His presence... And so I argue about the world; - *if* there be a God, *since* there is a God, the human race is implicated in some terrible aboriginal calamity. It is out of joint with the purposes of its Creator. This is a fact, a fact as true as the fact of its existence; and thus the doctrine of what is theologically called original sin becomes to me almost as certain as that the world exists, and as the existence of God."[21]

So temporal or historical evil and suffering entered the world with the Fall and original sin. The genre of Genesis 3 is literary history: "The account of the fall in *Genesis 3* uses figurative language, but affirms a primeval event, a deed that took place *at the beginning of the history of man*. Revelation gives us the certainty of faith that the whole of human history is marked by the original fault freely committed by our first parents" (CCC §390) that the Bible calls Adam and Eve.

In this connection, we can understand why John Paul says that "suffering cannot be divorced from the sin of the beginnings, from what St. John calls the 'sin of the world,' *from the sinful background* of the personal actions and social processes in human history." "[O]ne cannot reject the criterion that, at the basis of human suffering, there is a complex involvement with sin," the pope adds, "the sin that took root in this history both as an original inheritance and as the 'sin of the world' and as the sum of personal sins" (SD §15).

We live in a fallen world as a consequence of the original sin that amounts to the loss of our share in the divine life, or divine friendship, enjoyed by Adam and Eve, and thus of the integrity and immortality that stemmed from such sanctifying grace. Though John Paul urges us to exercise "great caution in judging man's suffering as a consequence of concrete sin" (ibid.), because there is no necessary connection between suffering and punishment, he nonetheless insists that humanity suffers as a result of the radical nature of our fall from sanctifying grace, which began with original sin and is extended through personal sins, indeed, through human nature. Human nature "is wounded in the natural powers proper to it; subject to ignorance, suffering, and the dominion of death; and inclined to sin—an inclination to evil that is called 'concupiscence'" (CCC §405).

Thus, in defeating the dominion of sin and death brought about by the Fall and original sin through the saving work of Christ, God gives human beings a new supernatural principle, which makes them a new creation, to replace that given them by original sin and this makes it possible for humanity to live anew in sanctifying grace. In short, the root of human suffering itself has been redeemed from the dominion of sin and death and raised to the level of redemption.

Christ's Redemptive Suffering

For our purposes here, then, the most important aspect of Christ's victory over sin and death is not only that, in his atoning work, he has taken upon himself the sins of all persons but *also their suffering.*

If I understand John Paul correctly, Christ in his suffering and death on the cross not only takes upon himself suffering in its fundamental and definitive sense, accomplishing our redemption through it; but also, he insists, Christ himself "in His redemptive suffering has become, in a certain sense, a sharer in all human sufferings" (SD §20). Again: "Christ through His own salvific suffering is very much present in every human suffering, and can act from within that suffering by the powers of His Spirit of Truth, His consoling Spirit" (SD §26). Still again: "Christ, the Incarnate Word, confirmed through his own life – in poverty, humiliation and toil—and especially through his passion and death, that God is with every person in his suffering. Indeed, God takes upon himself the multiform suffering of man's earthly existence. At the same time Jesus Christ reveals that this suffering possesses a redemptive and salvific value and power."[22]

In the next chapter, I will discuss the sense in which our suffering is redemptive when and only when it is united with the sufferings of Christ. For now, I continue giving an account of Christ's redemptive suffering.

The doctrine of God's suffering love goes beyond the hope of Romans 8 and touches present suffering itself. As Benedict Ashley explains this most important point:

> God the Father will wipe away our tears and give us ultimate and superabundant compensation in the future Kingdom. Yet he wishes us to achieve this not merely as a pure gift, but also as the just reward of our own achievements that because they are human necessarily involve pain and struggle. Human growth in knowledge, human growth in virtue, human transformation

of the world must be in the human mode that works dialectically through contrasts, struggle, courage and patience. Yet God understands that subjectively it is very hard for us to accept and endure this fact of actual, even necessary, suffering. The only way to make our suffering easier and ultimately to compensate it superabundantly is by sympathy not merely in the sense of appreciating our pain, *but of experiencing it himself with us. Immanuel, "God with us," Jesus Christ, has chosen to suffer and die with us and thus to enter into infinite delight through suffering with us.*[23]

Thus, God—in Christ—assumes all human suffering, being then, accordingly, a participant in our pain. Yet there is more: the Achilles' heel of the doctrine of God's suffering love, at least on some interpretations, is found in the question posed by Ashley: "if God is to suffer with us, how can we be assured that in the end we will be victorious with him?"[24]

This question is particularly troublesome for those who imply that God must undergo change given that he suffers with us. This conclusion limits God, taking away his omnipotence and our assurance that he can surely save us. Ashley's response to this question is illuminating:

> The doctrine of the Incarnation avoids this, since God the Father does not become incarnate, but only God the Son, and God the Son suffers with us not through his divine nature but through his assumed human nature that unlike his divinity is capable of suffering. But does not this mean that he does not really suffer, but only that his human nature suffers? No, because it is one and the same divine Person who is both God and human. The suffering of his human nature is his suffering, no one else's, just as my bodily suffering is my suffering although I am not just a body. Moreover, this incarnate Son is anointed with the Holy Spirit whom he sends upon the Church and the world as his infinite strengthening and consoling power, so that the God who truly suffers remains infinite in his power to save us.[25]

So, on the one hand, Christ suffers in our place humanity's godforsakenness, our abandonment by God, this suffering which is the separation, the rejection by the Father, the estrangement from him, which is the ultimate evil of, and thus the price paid for, the turning away from God that is contained in sin (SD §18). In this suffering we have the depth of Christ's sacrifice for us. As John Paul says, "Jesus knew that by this ultimate phase of His sacrifice, reaching the intimate core of His being, He completed the work of reparation which was the purpose of His sacrifice for the expiation of sins. If sin is separation from God, Jesus had to experience in the crisis of His union with the Father a suffering proportionate to that separation"(CoC, II, 473).

But contrary to the claim that we have here an "intradivine *theologia crucis*" in which "God is set against God,"[26] John Paul's account of Jesus Christ's suffering rests on a Chalcedonian Christology.[27] In an eloquent passage that bears quoting in full, John Paul II writes:

> Here we touch upon the duality of nature of a *single personal subject* of redemptive suffering. He who by His passion and death on the cross brings about the Redemption is the only-begotten Son whom God "gave." And at the same time this *Son who is consubstantial with the Father suffers as a man*. His suffering has human dimensions; it also has—unique in the history of humanity—a depth and intensity which, while being human, can also be an incomparable depth and intensity of suffering, insofar as the man who suffers is in person the only-begotten Son Himself; "God from God." Therefore, only He—the only-begotten Son—is capable of embracing the measure of evil contained in the sin of man: in every sin and in "total" sin, according to the dimensions of the historical existence of humanity on earth" (SD §17; my emphasis).[28]

Yet on the other hand, as Jacques Maritain has said, "It is indeed true that everything has been expiated by the suffering of Jesus alone, but as Head of Humanity, in communion with all other men, and [hence] recapitulating in Him all the sorrows of all other men." "There is but one single Cross," adds Maritain, "that of Jesus, in which all are called to participate. Jesus has taken on Him all the *sufferings* at the same time as all the *sins*, all the sufferings of the past, of the present, and of the future, gathered together, concentrated in Him as in a convergent mirror, in the instant that by His sacrifice He became—in a manner *fully consummated* and through the sovereign exercise of His liberty and of His love of man achieving in supreme obedience and supreme union the work which was entrusted to Him—the Head of humanity in the victory over sin" (GHJ, 41-42).

John Paul is getting at the same dimension of Christian soteriology in claiming that "Christ's passion and death pervade, redeem, and ennoble all human suffering, because through the Incarnation he desired to express his solidarity with humanity, which gradually opens to communion with him in faith and love" (CoC, II, 439). Here the pope states the crux of his interpretation:

> Behold, He, though innocent, takes upon Himself the sufferings of all people, because He takes upon Himself the sins of all. "The Lord has laid on him the iniquity of us all": *all* human sin in its breadth and depth becomes the true cause of the Redeemer's suffering. If the suffering 'is measured' by the evil suffered, then the words of the prophet [Isaiah] enable us to understand *the extent of this evil* and suffering with which Christ burdened Himself. It can be said that this is "substitutive" suffering; but above all it is "redemptive." The Man of Sorrows of that prophecy [of Isaiah] is truly that "Lamb of God who takes away the sin of the world." In His suffering, sins are cancelled out precisely because He alone as the only-begotten Son could take them upon Himself, accept them *with that love for the Father which overcomes* the evil of every sin [i.e., estrangement from God]; in a certain sense He annihilates this evil in the spiritual space of the relationship between God and humanity, and fills this space with good...This work, in the plan of eternal love, has a redemptive character (SD §§17, 16).

As I see it, both Maritain and John Paul II are suggesting here a distinctly Catholic interpretation of the meaning of human suffering in light of Christian soteriology. John Paul II develops this interpretation, as I will show below. This interpretation is not merely about our identifying with Christ, who through his passion and death, says the Pope, "is a divine model for all who suffer, especially for Christians who know and accept in faith the meaning and value of the cross." Of course we should follow the way of the cross, John Paul adds, because "The incarnate Word suffered according to the Father's plan so that we too 'should follow in his steps' (1 Pet 2:21). He suffered and taught us to suffer."[29]

But this is not the heart of his interpretation. Furthermore, it is also not merely about the future resurrection and heavenly glorification that finds its beginning in Christ's cross (Gal 6:14; Phil 3:10-11; Rom 8:17-18; 2 Cor 4:17-18; 1 Pet 4:13). "Christ's resurrection has revealed 'the glory of the future age; and, at the same time, has confirmed 'the boast of the cross': the *glory that is hidden in the very suffering of Christ*" (SD §22). Nor is it merely about the triumphant love of God in Christ Jesus from which the very worst of human sufferings cannot separate us (Rom 8:31-39). Of course the Pope understands well the evangelical motif of suffering and glory, especially with reference to the cross and resurrection.

As he says, "The resurrection became, first of all, the manifestation of glory, which corresponds to Christ's being lifted up through the cross. If, in fact, the cross was to human eyes Christ's *emptying of Himself,* at the same time it was in the eyes of God *His being lifted up*. On the cross, Christ attained and fully accomplished His mission: by fulfilling the will of the Father, He at the same time fully realized Himself. In weakness He manifested His *power*, and in humiliation He manifested all *His messianic greatness*." (SD §22).

This interpretation is also not merely about what the pope calls the "Gospel *paradox of weakness and strength*" (SD §23; 2 Cor 12:9; 2 Tim 1:12; Phil 4:13). In other words, Christ experiences the core and summit of human weakness and powerlessness in being nailed to the cross and, nevertheless, in his weakness he is lifted up, confirmed by the power of the resurrection.

Similarly, "the weaknesses of all human suffering are capable of being infused with the same power of God manifested in Christ's cross." "In such a concept," John Paul adds, "*to suffer* means to become particularly *susceptible*, particularly *open to the working of the salvific powers of God*, offered to humanity in Christ" (SD §23).[30] Only one who is open to the saving powers of God can hear and act on the Word of

God: "My grace is sufficient for you, for my power is made perfect in weakness" (2 Cor 12:9-11).

What, then, does John Paul II have particularly in mind when insisting that "the victory over sin and death achieved by Christ is His cross and resurrection...*throws a new light* upon every suffering: the light of salvation. This is the light of the Gospel, that is, of the Good News." Christ strikes, he says, "at the very roots of human evil and thus draw[s] close in a salvific way to the whole world of suffering in which man shares" (SD §15).

God the Father's love for us is most perfectly revealed on the Cross of Jesus Christ, where God the Son suffers all that we can suffer. Says Ashley, "Looking at him and believing that he is now at the Father's right hand sending the Holy Spirit upon us, our own present suffering is united with his. While it remains human pain, it is transformed by the hope of glory, a hope that is not merely future but present in the infinite power of God in Christ. And as Christ by his suffering saved the world, so by our suffering with him we save each other."[31]

What does Ashley mean by saying that by suffering with Christ we save each other? Of course he doesn't think that Christ's atoning work was somehow insufficient to save all men and that by sharing in Christ's suffering we contribute to the salvation of others.

I shall return to this question of our redemptive suffering in the next chapter when considering the meaning of Colossians 1:24. I will address two obvious questions. First, what sense can be given to the notion that Christ takes the whole world of human suffering upon his very self? Second, what sound theological sense can be given to the notion that by uniting our suffering with Christ's Passion we fulfill a role that God has given us, namely, to participate in the historical outworking of God's plan of salvation for the whole human race, which was accomplished in and through the finished work of Christ on the cross?

Notes

1. White, *The Light of Christ: An Introduction to Catholicism*, 168-69.
2. For a brief catechesis of Christ's redemptive death in God's plan of salvation, see the *Catechism of the Catholic Church*, §§599-618.
3. McGrath, *Intellectuals Don't Need God*, 135-37.

4. Ibid., 137.

5. Several paragraphs in this chapter are taken from my book, *Pope Francis, The Legacy of Vatican II*, Chapter 3, "Mercy and Justice Meet at the Cross."

6. Walter Cardinal Kasper, Mercy, *The Essence of the Gospel and the Key to Christian Life*. Reformed theologian G.C. Berkouwer correctly notes, "Certainly, in both the Old and New Testament we read of God's wrath—against His own people as well as against His enemies—but it is nowhere detached from the perfect holiness which reacts against guilt. That explains that His wrath may attain tremendous proportions, and yet altogether lacks the traits of the demonic, so that in repentance and faith there is always a way to turn from wrath to grace. . . . In this turning from wrath to grace God's sovereignty is recognized. This turning is never a matter of course, but is experienced and acknowledged as mercy, precisely because of its freedom. That is why the preaching of God's wrath—no matter what proportions it assumes—never affects the basis of one's trust whenever this trust rediscovers the way to God's heart in experiencing His judgment and its righteousness" (*Divine Election*, 91). John R.W. Stott writes, "God's wrath in the words of Dr. Leon Morris is his 'personal divine revulsion to evil' and his 'personal vigorous opposition' to it. To speak thus of God's anger is a legitimate anthropomorphism, provided that we recognize it as no more than a rough and ready parallel, since God's anger is absolutely pure and uncontaminated by those elements that render human anger sinful. Human anger is usually arbitrary and uninhibited; divine anger is always principled and controlled. Our anger tends to be a spasmodic outburst, aroused by pique and seeking revenge; God's is a continuous, settled antagonism, aroused only by evil and expressed in its condemnation. God is entirely free from personal animosity or vindictiveness; indeed, he is sustained simultaneously with undiminished love for the offender" (*The Cross of Christ*, 107).

7. Pope's Homily at Vespers on Eve of New Year [2015]," Vatican City, 31 December 2014: http://www.zenit.org/en/articles/pope-s-homily-at-vespers-on-eve-of-new-year.

8. "Wrath," entry in *Dictionary of Biblical Theology*, Updated Second Edition, 683-688, and for this quotation, 683. See also the entry, "Wrath," in *Sacramentum Verbi, An Encyclopedia of Biblical Theology*, 1006-1011. Especially illuminating is G.C. Berkouwer, *Sin*, Chapter 11, "Sin, Wrath, and Forgiveness," 354-423.

9. Berkouwer, *Sin*, 39.

10. Ratzinger, *The Yes of Jesus Christ*, 94-95.

11. Idem, *Introduction to Christianity*, 282-83.

12. Kasper, *Mercy*, 75: "With the idea of substitutionary atonement, it is not . . . a matter of a vengeful God needing a victim so that his wrath can be assuaged. On the contrary, by willing the death of his Son on account of his mercy, God takes back his wrath and provides space for his mercy and thereby also for life. By taking our place in and through his son, he takes the life-destroying effects of sin upon himself in order to bestow upon us life-anew. 'So if anyone is in Christ, there is a new creation; everything old has passed away; see, everything has become new!' (2 Cor 5:17). It is not we who can reconcile God with us. He is the one who has

reconciled himself with us (2 Cor 5:18)."

13. J. Murray, *Redemption—Accomplished and Applied*, 37-38.

14. Fundamental to my thinking on this question is John Paul II, *Dives in Misericordia*. See also, Berkouwer, *The Work of Christ*, 277.

15. I am grateful to Gustavo Martin for reminding me of this important point.

16. Ashley, *Choosing a World-View and Value-System: An Ecumenical Apologetics*, 316.

17. Nichols, *The Shape of Catholic Theology*, 72.

18. *CoC*, vol. II, 17-77. On original sin as universal sinfulness, see 33-34, 36-37, 39, 41, and 46; on natural sinfulness, see pp. 28, 30; on inherited sinfulness, see 28, 36-37, 39-43, 45-46, 48, and 55; on Adamic sinfulness, see 23-27, 41, 43, 44-4, 48, and 60. See also, *CCC*, §§396-406. I have profited much from Henri Blocher, *Original Sin: Illuminating the Riddle*, especially 15-35. See also Geach, *Providence and Evil*, especially Chapter 5, 84-101.

19. Nichols, *Epiphany: A Theological Introduction to Catholicism*, 175-76. Pope John Paul upholds the essential historicity of the Fall in Vol. II of *A Catechesis on the Creed*: "The description of the first sin, which we find in the third chapter of Genesis, acquires a greater clarity in the context of creation and of the bestowal of gifts. By these gifts, God constituted man in the state of holiness and of original justice. This description hinges on the transgression of the divine command not to eat 'of the fruit of the tree of the knowledge of good and evil.' This is to be interpreted by taking into account the character of the ancient text and especially its literary form. However, while bearing in mind this scientific requirement in the study of the first book of Sacred Scripture, it cannot be denied that one sure element emerges from the detailed account of the sin. It describes a primordial event, that is, a fact, which according to revelation took place at the beginning of human history" (27). If I'm not mistaken, what the pope is saying in this citation is similar to the point made by Henri Blocher, "The real issue when we try to interpret Genesis 2-3 is not whether we have a historical account of the fall, but whether or not we may read it as the account of a historical fall. The problem is not historiography as a genre narrowly defined—in annals, chronicles, or even saga—but correspondence with discrete realities in our ordinary space and sequential time" (*Original Sin*, 50). See also, T.C. O'Brien, O.P., who writes, "Original sin is taken on the level of a *history* of salvation, and the state and the sin of Adam are treated as real events and parts of a divine plan, *economy*, for man. To regard the first sin and the fall as a mere symbol or mythological representation of men's collectivity in their sinful condition is incompatible with Catholic teaching, which envisages a real situation of a real person, namely a 'sin' actually committed by an individual together with its consequences for him." Again: "All the literary forms are shaped and directed to bring out as history God's plan of man's creation, fall and redemption. There is a real link between past events, under whatever literary form they appear, and the conditions present to the author and explained in the light of these origins. Unlike the ancient myths these Biblical accounts are not a symbolic expression of some universal truth; they are an account of an actual situation in terms of its causes: the present is seen in the past, the past in the present" (Ap-

pendix 3 and 4, respectively, in Volume 26, *Original Sin,* of St. Thomas Aquinas, *Summa Theologiae* 1a2ae. 81-85, at 115, 121).

20. Oakes, "Original Sin," 23. See also *CoC* vol. II: "Finally the whole of human existence on earth is subject to the fear of death, which according to revelation is clearly connected with original sin. Sin itself is synonymous with spiritual death, because through sin man has lost sanctifying grace, the source of supernatural life. The sign and consequence of original sin is bodily death, such as it has been experienced since that time by all humanity. Man was created by God for immortality. Death appears as a tragic leap in the dark, and is the consequence of sin, as if by an immanent logic but especially as the punishment of God. Such is the teaching of revelation and such is the faith of the Church" (50-51).

21. Newman, *Apologia Pro Vita Sua,* part VII, 218.

22. John Paul II, *Catechesis on the Creed,* vol. I, 274. Elsewhere the Holy Father says, "The Gospel of suffering signifies not only the presence of suffering in the Gospel, as one of the themes of the Good News, but also the revelation of the salvific power and salvific significance of suffering in Christ's messianic mission and, subsequently, in the mission and vocation of the Church" (SD §25).

23. Ashley, *Choosing a World-View,* 317.

24. Ibid.

25. Ibid., 317-18.

26. Dupre, "Philosophy and the Mystery of Evil," 60.

27. Karol Wojtyla writes, "He suffered therefore in all the mystery of his Person, in all the indescribable depth of his nature as God-man, the one and only subject and the one and only author of redemption of the world" (*Sign of Contradiction,* 71). In the background of John Paul II's account of Jesus Christ's suffering is a Chalcedonian Christology. On the relevance of Chalcedonian Christology for the problem of evil, see Marilyn McCord Adams, "Chalcedonian Christology: A Christian Solution to the Problem of Evil," in *Philosophy and Theology Discourse,* 173-98. Heinrich Denzinger, *Compendium of Creeds, Definitions, and Declarations on Matters of Faith and Morals,* §§300-302 Chalcedonian Creed (A.D. 451): "Following therefore the holy Fathers, we unanimously teach to confess one and the same Son, our Lord Jesus Christ, the same perfect in divinity and perfect in humanity, the same truly God and truly man composed of rational and body, the same one in being with the Father as to the divinity an done in being with us, as to humanity, like unto us in all things but sin *[cf. Heb 4:15].* The same was begotten from the Father before the ages as to the divinity and in the latter days for us and our salvation was born as to his humanity from Mary the Virgin Mother of God. <We confess that> one and the same Lord Jesus Christ, the only begotten Son, must be acknowledged in two natures, without confusion or change, without division or separation. The distinction between the natures was never abolished by their union but rather the character proper to each of the two natures was preserved as they came together in one Person and one hypostasis. He is not split or divided into two Persons, but he is one and the same only begotten Son, God the Word, the Lord Jesus Christ, as formerly the prophets and later Jesus Christ

himself have taught us about him and as has been handed down to us by the creed of the Fathers."

28. Twenty years later in his 2001 Apostolic Letter, *Novo Millennio Ineunte*, John Paul II affirms that Christ's suffering rests on a Chalcedonian Christology. "Jesus' cry on the Cross, dear Brothers and Sisters, is not the cry of anguish of a man without hope, but the prayer of the Son who offers his life to the Father in love, for the salvation of all. At the very moment when he identifies with our sin, 'abandoned' by the Father, he 'abandons' himself into the hands of the Father. His eyes remain fixed on the Father. Precisely because of the knowledge and experience of the Father which he alone has, even at this moment of darkness he sees clearly the gravity of sin and suffers because of it. He alone, who sees the Father and rejoices fully in him, can understand completely what it means to resist the Father's love by sin. More than an experience of physical pain, his Passion is an agonizing suffering of the soul. Theological tradition has not failed to ask how Jesus could possibly experience at one and the same time his profound unity with the Father, by its very nature a source of joy and happiness, and an agony that goes all the way to his final cry of abandonment. The simultaneous presence of these two seemingly irreconcilable aspects is rooted in the fathomless depths of the hypostatic union" (§26).

29. *CoC*, II, 439-40. In *SD*, John Paul says, "Christ's sufferings" have "the power of a supreme example" (§22). In this light, we can understand the claim that "Suffering is also an invitation to manifest the moral greatness of man, his *spiritual maturity*." That is, the "*spiritual tempering* of man in the midst of trials and tribulations, which is the particular vocation of those who share in Christ's suffering...Suffering, as it were, contains a special *call to the virtue* which man must exercise on his own part. And this is the virtue of perseverance in bearing whatever disturbs and causes him harm. In doing this, the individual unleashes hope which maintains in him the conviction that suffering will not get the better of him, that it will not deprive him of his dignity as a human being, a dignity linked to awareness of the meaning of life" (§23).

30. The pope is not suggesting that in our suffering we literally experience a share of Christ's pain, or mystically identify with the "inner life of God," because Christ "Himself in His redemptive suffering has become, in a certain sense, a sharer in all human suffering" (SD §20). Marilyn McCord Adams sketches these and other possible interpretations of suffering in light of Christian soteriology in "Horrendous Evils," 218-19; see also 161-73.

31. Ashley, *Choosing a World-View*, 318. The phrase "we save each other" is potentially misleading. It suggests the heresy of Pelagianism, meaning thereby the teaching "that human beings can achieve salvation through their own sustained efforts" (*A Concise Dictionary of Theology*, edited by O'Collins and Farrugia, 176). Of course I am not suggesting that Fr. Benedict Ashley had this meaning in mind.

CHAPTER 4

Redemptive Suffering

Sharers in the Sufferings of Christ

Scourged, mocked with a crown of thorns, [Jesus] carried to Mount Calvary together with the weight of his cross the truth of human suffering, humiliation, scorn, torture, agony, death. . . . On the day of his death Jesus entered into the fullest and deepest communion and solidarity with the entire human family, and especially with all those who throughout history have been the victims of injustice, cruelty and scornful abuse.[1]

St. Paul wrote, "I rejoice in my sufferings [*pathemasi*, noun from *paschō*] for your sake, and in my flesh I am filling up what is lacking in Christ's afflictions [*thlipsis*] for the sake of his body, that is, the church" (Col 1:24). This passage should be read in light of another passage of St. Paul:

Blessed be the God and Father of our Lord Jesus Christ, the Father of mercies and God of all comfort, who comforts us in all our affliction, so that we may be able to comfort those who are in any affliction, with the comfort with which we ourselves are comforted by God. For as we share abundantly in Christ's sufferings, so through Christ we share abundantly in comfort too. If we are afflicted, it is for your comfort and salvation; and if we are comforted, it is for your comfort, which you experience when you patiently endure the same sufferings that we suffer. Our hope for you is unshaken, for we know that as you share in our sufferings, you will also share in our comfort. (2 Cor 1:3-7)

Much of this chapter is taken up with making theological sense of the notion of redemptive suffering in light of these two Pauline verses. Two particular questions are at stake in understanding its meaning. One, what is the meaning of filling up what is lacking; and, accordingly, how should we understand the meaning of "Christ's afflictions (*thlipsis*)"? Two, how should we understand the sense that sharing in Christ's sufferings brings his comfort and salvation, Christ's merciful and all-encompassing love, to others who are suffering?

Regarding the first, I think we must say that nothing has been lacking in the atoning work of Christ, and hence neither Paul nor you nor I can supplement or complete it. Patrick Rogers puts this point well: "As expiatory sacrifice the passion of Christ was [singularly] unique, perfect and all-sufficient; here Paul would perfectly agree with the epistle to the Hebrews, that the sacrifice of Christ was 'once for all' (Heb 9:26), and cannot be shared by any other 'mediator'."[2]

We must, then, distinguish between *objective* redemption and *subjective* redemption. Objective redemption is a finished matter, an accomplished fact: the scope of Christ's atoning work is sufficient for the salvation of all men, although efficacious only for those who participate in its saving benefits.[3] Subjective redemption—the infinite merits of Christ's atoning work are applied to us—is the on-going sanctification and hence the fruition of uniting our sufferings with Christ's sufferings. There is a difference between sharing in the sufferings of Christ and uniting our sufferings with his sufferings.[4]

The question arises here whether we are participating in Christ's very suffering on the cross. John Paul II explains that sharing in Christ's suffering gives one "the certainty that in the spiritual dimension of the work of Redemption *he* [the one who suffers] *is serving*, like Christ, *the salvation of his brothers and sisters*" (SD §27). How does sharing in the redemptive sufferings of Christ's sacrifice assist in the salvation of the world by bringing to fruition the work of Redemption? This question raised by the concluding sentence of the John Paul passage brings us back to the same point made by Ashley at the conclusion of the last chapter, and hence to the same two questions I then raised.

As to the first question, what sense can be given to the notion that Christ takes the whole world of human suffering upon his very self? Does John Paul mean to say that Christ actually experienced in his suffering and death on the cross, as humanity's head, which is his body, the Church, the past, present, and future sufferings of all human beings who belong to the Church in which Christ continues to live in the Holy Spirit? Did Christ actually experience the suffering of my granddaughter Penelope? Yes, that is precisely what he is saying: the Son of God, Jesus, the Crucified, has taken upon himself the sufferings of all people and offered them up, in loving obedience, to his Father for the supreme good of the redemption of the world (SD §18).

Maritain puts John Paul's point about Jesus entering into the fullest and deepest communion and solidarity with all the sufferings of human beings as follows: because Christ suffered our sufferings "He has rendered all these sufferings meritorious of eternal life, holy and redemptive *in themselves*, and co-redemptive *in the Church*, which is both His Spouse and His Mystical Body" (GHJ, 42) In short, then, the vicarious suffering of Jesus on the Cross has redeemed human suffering itself. So not only is redemption accomplished through the suffering of Christ, but suffering itself, says John Paul, "has entered into a completely new dimension and a new order: *it has been linked to love*, to that love which Christ spoke to Nicodemus [John 3:16], to that love which creates good, drawing it out by means of suffering, just as the supreme good of the Redemption of the world was drawn from the cross of Christ, and from that cross constantly takes its beginning" (SD §18).

Having made his own the sufferings of all people, this suffering has a redemptive power. As Jacques Maritain says, "we are no longer alone in bearing our sufferings (we had never been, but we have known this only when He came). He has borne our sufferings before us, and He put into them together with grace and charity, a salvific power and the seed of transfiguration" (GHJ, 42). Thus, the answer to the question about suffering and its meaning is Jesus's own suffering on the cross (see SD §18). Objectively speaking, Jesus has taken the whole world of human suffering upon himself, and hence that suffering has salvific power that we can draw on as we, in union with Christ, "continue to work out our salvation with fear and trembling, for it is God who works in you to will and to act according to his purpose" (Phil 2:12-13).

There is an obvious question: If human suffering has been redeemed, why has God not abolished the mass of sufferings engendered by original sin and our own personal sins? As I asked in Chapter 3, "Why has an all-powerful God permitted us to suffer so much *here and now?* Why has he not eliminated the suffering and simply given us happiness that after all is ultimately his gift to give?" Maritain's reply, and the answer of John Paul as well, is that "human suffering is not abolished, because men, by the blood of Christ and the merits of Christ *in which they participate*, are with Him the co-authors of their [on-going] salvation" (GHJ, 42). How do we participate in Christ's sufferings on the cross? Co-authors, or, more precisely, cooperators, does not mean that God does part of the work of salvation and man does the rest. Rather, since Christ has already taken upon himself the sufferings all men, then co-authors mean that we are working out our salvation in union with his sufferings. This cooperation is itself not only an effect of grace,[5] rather than an action arising from man's innate powers, but also it means that by sharing in the infinite value of the cross of the suffering Christ we are freeing the "present life from the results of the bonds of sin."[6]

This brings us to the second question I raised above, namely, the theological sense that can be given to the notion that by our suffering being united with Christ's sufferings we participate in the historical outworking of God's plan of salvation. Contrary to Calvin, this question does not presume that a man's sufferings in and of themselves, and hence apart from being united with the sufferings of Christ, expiate the sins of men.[7]

Rather, we share in Christ's suffering in such a way that our suffering, too, is redemptive, and even essential to furthering the plan of salvation, not in the sense of course that we can add anything to Christ's infinite merits and to his blood, says Maritain, but rather in the sense that through our suffering and our love we apply the inexhaustible and infinite merits that Christ won for us on the cross (GHJ, 42). These merits have infinite value. They can never be exhausted. As the *Catechism of the Catholic Church* states, "They were offered so that the whole of mankind could be set free from sin and attain communion with the Father. In Christ, the Redeemer himself, the satisfaction and merits of his Redemption exist and find their efficacy" (CCC §1476). Subjective redemption is, then, not an extension of the infinite merits of Christ's sufferings, objective redemption, but rather an application of those merits to us.

John Paul II develops this very same line of interpretation. All people, says the pope, are *"called to share in that suffering* through which the Redemption was accomplished." They are called, he adds, "to share in that suffering through which all human suffering has also been redeemed. In bringing about the Redemption through suffering, Christ has also *raised human suffering to the level of Redemption.* Thus each man, in his suffering, can also become a sharer in the redemptive suffering of Christ" (SD §19). In other words, "insofar as man becomes a sharer in Christ's sufferings—in any part of the world and at any time in history—to that extent *he in his own way completes* the suffering through which Christ accomplished the Redemption of the world" (SD §24). There are two important things to keep in mind here in order to understand what John Paul is saying.

First, objective redemption is a finished matter, an accomplished fact: the scope of Christ's atoning work is sufficient for the salvation of all men, although efficacious only for those who participate in its saving benefits. So, the pope is not suggesting that we are adding anything to that work of redemption. What does it, then, mean to share in Christ's sufferings? Through mystical union in faith with Christ we are indwelt by the third person of the Holy Trinity, the Holy Spirit. "God's love has been poured into our hearts through the Holy Spirit which has been given to us" (Rom 5:5). Christ is in us and we are in him as sharers of God's life in Christ through the agency of the Holy Spirit. In this union, I discover that my sufferings are already Christ's and therefore are "enriched with a new content and meaning" (SD §20). Second, then, since Christ has taken the suffering of all men upon himself, when we unite our suffering with his sufferings, to work out our salvation means that we are continually working to bring the infinite merits of Christ's suffering to fruition in our lives through the process of sanctification.

Furthermore, the incomparable good of union with God in heaven compensates all the finite evils we suffer here (Rom 8:18). The ultimate meaning of suffering and death is revealed in the resurrection of Jesus Christ. Says St. Paul, "For if we have been united with him in a death like his, we shall certainly be united with him in a resurrection like his…But if we have died with Christ, we believe that we shall also live with him" (Rom 6:5, 8). Germain Grisez makes this point well: "Just as Jesus willingly suffered, because he looked forward to the joy of resurrection (see Heb 12:2), so Christians who are faithful can anticipate glory even amidst sufferings, and so can honestly say: 'When we cry, "Abba,

Father," it is that very Spirit bearing witness with our spirit that we are children of God, and if children then heirs, heirs of God and joint heirs with Christ—if, in fact, we suffer with Him so that we may also be glorified with him' (Rom 8:15-17)."[8]

Yet there is still more: we walk in newness of life here and now. "We were buried therefore with him by baptism into death, so that as Christ was raised from the dead by the glory of the Father, we too might walk in newness of life" (Rom 6:4). In other words, we are united with a resurrected, living Christ, and from this mystical union with this living Christ we have the high calling of bringing forth fruit to God. As one author puts it, "Christ is the vine, and we are the branches, abiding in him, bringing forth fruit."[9]

This brings us to a second point. Most important, as a sharer in the sufferings of Christ, I discover through faith that in uniting my sufferings, in loving obedience, to Christ's sacrifice I am furthering the glory of God and his plan of salvation. Says John Paul, "For, *whoever suffers in union with Christ*—just as the Apostle Paul bears his 'tribulations' in union with Christ—not only receives from Christ that strength already referred to but also 'completes' by his suffering 'what is lacking in Christ's afflictions [for the sake of his body, that is, the Church]' (Col 1:24)" (SD §24). Here, too, we meet the troublesome word "complete," and the question arises again as to whether the pope is suggesting that I am adding to Christ's sufferings, as if it takes my suffering and Christ's sufferings—the two together—to make up the full sum.[10]

Let us look again briefly at the entire verse in St. Paul's letter to the Colossians that plays a key role here in John Paul's interpretation of God's suffering love. "Now I rejoice in my sufferings for your sake, and in my flesh I complete what is lacking in Christ's afflictions for the sake of his body, that is the church." Again, is the pope suggesting that the atoning work of Christ is still incomplete? Of course not: John Paul never wavers from insisting that nothing is lacking in the *finished* work of Christ on the cross. In fact, he knows that *thlipsis* (afflictions) is never used of the cross, and, significantly, the word used of Christ's sufferings is almost always a form of *paschō* (noun pl, *pathēmata*).[11] Furthermore, Christ explicitly said of his sacrifice, "it is finished," it is accomplished (John 19:30). Nothing can be added and nothing need be added to his merits—they are of infinite value—and to his atoning blood. Christ's actual death is ontologically sufficient, complete and once-for-all. Christ's sufferings are inexhaustible and infinite in their merit and saving power. But, then, what could St. Paul mean? What are Christ's afflictions? How are they insufficient?

As New Testament scholar Eduard Schweizer says, "The decisive question in this case is that of the meaning of 'Christ's afflictions.'" He reminds us, "This expression is never used in the New Testament for the Passion, nor for Jesus' experience of suffering in general." Rather, Christ's afflictions in this verse refer to the "sufferings endured in the community for the sake of Christ, or 'in Christ.' …If one understands the sentence thus, then the point is that the 'afflictions of Christ' are only endured in a way that still lacks something, that is, that they are not yet complete; but that 'Christ's afflictions' are…still outstanding."[12] Thus, if Schweizer is right in his exegesis of this verse then Christ's afflictions refer to "what is yet to come of the afflictions of the (corporate) Christ."[13]

The corporate Christ is His Body. And since the body of Christ, the Church, is incorporated with Christ as its head, and is one with him, their sufferings are his, and his are theirs. In other words, these afflictions are incomplete because we still have our whole lives ahead of us and in our life's journey with the Lord we know that there will be suffering and concomitant afflictions in living the Christian life, and the latter belong to Christ.[14] Says Ashley, "The doctrine of the Incarnation includes the Church as the Body of Christ in that Jesus continues to be present really, though sacramentally…Our consolation, therefore, is in the companionship of the suffering Christ present in our fellow Christians, the Church. We bear a common witness and carry on a common struggle that we believe and experience to be a share in Christ's sufferings, endowed with the power of transforming ourselves and the world."[15] As John Paul elaborates in an important passage:

> The suffering of Christ created the good of the world's Redemption. This good in itself is inexhaustible and infinite. No man can add anything to it. But at the same time, in the mystery of the Church as His Body, Christ has in a sense opened His own redemptive suffering to all human suffering. Insofar as man becomes a sharer in Christ's sufferings… to that extent he in his

own way completes the suffering through which Christ accomplished the Redemption of the world. Does this mean that the Redemption achieved by Christ is not complete? No. It only means that Redemption, accomplished through satisfactory love, *remains always open to all love* expressed in *human suffering*. In this dimension – the dimension of love – the Redemption that has already been completely accomplished is, in a certain sense, constantly being accomplished. Christ achieved the Redemption completely and to the very limit; but at the same time He did not bring it to a close. In this redemptive suffering, through which the Redemption of the world was accomplished, Christ opened Himself from the beginning to every human suffering and constantly does so. Yes, it seems to be part *of the very essence of Christ's redemptive suffering* that this suffering requires to be unceasingly completed…[This Redemption] lives and develops as the Body of Christ, the Church, and in this dimension every human suffering, by reason of the loving union with Christ, completes the suffering of Christ. It completes that suffering *just as the Church completes the redemptive work of Christ*. The mystery of the Church—that body which completes in itself also Christ's crucified and risen body—indicates at the same time the space or context in which human sufferings complete the sufferings of Christ.[16]

It should be clear that the pope is not claiming that individuals earn their salvation by the works of suffering. We complete Christ's sufferings, and the Church accordingly completes Christ's redemptive work, only in the sense of bringing it to fruition in a man's life. Salvation is through the finished work of Christ only. Yet suffering is an indispensable element in the redemption that was initiated, finished, and merited by Christ. Christ wants us to collaborate in his plan of salvation, and that plan includes his taking upon himself the sufferings of all men, and hence our sufferings, when offered up in love, uniting our sufferings to his all-sufficient suffering, can be of benefit to ourselves and others.

This emphasis is not incompatible with the gratuity of grace. As

Hans Urs von Balthasar says, "Even suffering, *particularly* suffering, is a precious gift that the one suffering can hand on to others; it helps, it purifies, it atones, it communicates divine graces. The sufferings of a mother can bring a wayward son back to the right path; the sufferings of someone with cancer or leprosy, if ordered to God, can be a capital for God to use, bearing fruit in the most unexpected places. Suffering, accepted with thankfulness and handed on, participates in the great fruitfulness of everything that streams from God's joy and returns to him by circuitous paths."[17] It is through the overflowing, superabundant fullness of grace won by the cross of Christ, not because of any flaw, imperfection, or incompleteness, that a calling is given to us in the work of redemption.[18] "Suffering is," says John Paul, "a vocation; it is a calling to accept the burden of pain in order to transform it into a sacrifice of purification and of reconciliation offered to the Father in Christ and with Christ, for one's own salvation and that of others."[19] Fellowship in Christ's sufferings (Phil 3:10), in and through the Church, Christ's Body, is the only way to hear his answer to the question of the meaning of suffering.

Conversion to the Gospel of Suffering

We continue to write new chapters of the gospel of suffering in our Christian lives whenever we suffer together with Christ, in loving union with his salvific sufferings. This is how I have experienced my sufferings resulting from the loss of my beloved granddaughter Penelope. Conversion is required to discover not only the salvific meaning of suffering, but above all to discover the calling that Christ gives us to collaborate in his work of redemption by suffering together with him, uniting our sufferings to his redemptive sufferings.

This conversion does not lead us to think that in itself suffering is a good thing. No, says John Paul, "Suffering is, in itself, an experience of evil. But Christ has made suffering the firmest basis of the definitive good, namely the good of eternal salvation" (SD §26). Rather, we discover the positive value of suffering only when it is united to the sufferings of the crucified Christ. As John Paul says, "Ever since Christ chose the cross and died on Golgotha, all who suffer, especially those who suffer without fault, can come face to face with the 'holy one who suffers.' They can find in his passion the complete truth about suffering, its full meaning and its importance. In the light of this truth, all those who suffer can feel called to share in the work of redemption accomplished by means of the cross" (CoC, II, 456).

This kind of suffering bears witness to an interior maturity and spiritual greatness. As the Holy Father says, "This interior maturity and spiritual greatness in suffering are certainly the *result* of a particular *conversion* and cooperation with the grace of the crucified Redeemer. It is He Himself who acts at the heart of human sufferings through His Spirit of Truth, through the consoling Spirit. It is He who transforms, in a certain sense, the very substance of the spiritual life, indicating for the person who suffers a place close to Himself. *It is He*—as the interior Master and Guide—*who reveals* to the suffering brother and sister *this wonderful interchange*, situated at the very heart of the mystery of Redemption...For suffering cannot be *transformed* and changed by the grace from the outside, but *from within*" (SD §26).

This process of sanctification may be lengthy, helping one to overcome the sense of the uselessness of suffering and thereby progressively bring oneself closer to hearing Christ's answer to the meaning of suffering and, with it, to the ultimate goal of union with God. This process does not bring suffering to an end but only teaches us *how* to suffer.[20] "A source of joy is found in the *overcoming of the sense of the uselessness of suffering* . . . .The discovery of the salvific meaning of suffering in union with Christ *transforms* this depressing *feeling*" (SD §27).

This interior process of conversion is often set in motion by a typically human protest—it's unfair, indeed cruel, that I will be without my child the rest of my life—and, with it, the question why. This protest is impelled by the perception that there does not seem to be a morally sufficient reason why God would permit these evils to actually occur. We are looking for some meaning to our suffering, and usually we are searching for that meaning on the human level. In particular, we have a sense that suffering is useless; this sense not only tends to engulf us, but it makes us a burden to others. Says John Paul, "The person feels condemned to receive help and assistance from others, and at the same time seems useless to himself" (SD §27). We can overcome this feeling of uselessness by sharing in the redemptive suffering of Christ.

An obvious question is now this: how does discovering the redemptive meaning of suffering in union with Christ transform this feeling of uselessness? In this chapter, I have tried to show John Paul II's answer to this question. Perhaps even more basic is the question why God uses suffering to lead us to recognize, in some way, the sacrifice of Christ on the cross and, ultimately, to acknowledge and follow him. This question arises because the pope suggests that "it is suffering, more than anything else, which clears the way for the grace which transforms human souls" (SD §27). We know that individuals' souls need transformation because of their sinful character. But why choose suffering, more than anything else, as the instrument that makes us receptive or inclines a person to sanctifying grace?

The Holy Father does not say exactly, but I think we can surmise that his answer would be no different than the answer C. S. Lewis gives in *The Problem of Pain*: pain and suffering of all sorts are God's instrument for getting the rebellious self to lay down its arms. God allows the evil of suffering, then, only because it may produce a benefit for the sufferer. Put differently, they are "destined to prepare the way for a deeper love for God. So long as God does not take the cross from us, we must feel it as a participation in the Cross of Christ, as a costly treasure, as a divine gift of mysterious fruitfulness. In bearing our cross, we are placed in contact with Christ's suffering out of charity."[21]

Now, God either could not provide this benefit without the suffering, or at least suffering, more than anything else, seems the best means for attaining that benefit. As Benedict Ashley explains in a passage well worth quoting in full:

> If the end of the universe and its greatest good is for intelligent and free creatures to come to share knowingly and freely in God's life of self-giving love, then it is understandable why a loving God may permit them to sin if they freely so choose. This will be true, if only in this way they can from their own experience come to know best what God's love means in their lives. Thus the whole of human history can be understood as a school of love in that the lessons are not taught abstractly but from the experience of life lived in freedom. Because human beings only learn perfectly from actual experience and experience means they learn best from the contrast of good and evil, it is clearer why God has cho-

sen this pedagogy. Is it not a fact that for humans, love
in its fullest sense is never achieved without a struggle
between the lovers, without offense and forgiveness?[22]

John Paul directs his attention to the question regarding the meaning
of our suffering. We often put this question to God-in-Christ. Christ
replies from the cross, says the Holy Father, which is the heart of his
own suffering. "It often takes time, even a long time, for this answer to
begin to be interiorly perceived" (SD §26). John Paul is sensitive to the
individualized dynamics involved in coming to the interior perception
that sharing in the sufferings of Christ is the only way to hear Christ's
saving answer to the question of my suffering. What is it that I hear?
"Faith in sharing in the suffering of Christ brings with it the interior
certainty that the suffering person 'completes what is lacking in Christ's
afflictions'; the certainty that in the spiritual dimension of the work of
Redemption *he is serving*, like Christ, *the salvation of his brothers and sisters*. Therefore, he is carrying out an irreplaceable service." In some way,
and it is a mystery that we shall never grasp in this life: in the mystical
body of Christ, the sufferings of one member, when offered up in love,
can be of benefit to another. As Saint Paul wrote: "If we are afflicted, it
is for your comfort and salvation" (2 Cor 1:5).

This answer to the problem of my suffering does not refute all objections. Says John Paul II, "Christ does not answer directly and He does
not answer in the abstract this human questioning about the meaning
of suffering...The answer which comes through this sharing [in the sufferings of Christ], by way of interior encounter with the Master, is in
itself *something more than the mere abstract answer* to the question about
the meaning of suffering." If I understand the Holy Father correctly,
that we do not receive an abstract answer to our question implies that
Christ's answer does not cover all evils at once; and it certainly does not
focus on generic and global goods in the face of many and great evils.

The Holy Father's approach is a more person-centered one. Christ
replies by calling us to a vocation and those who follow it must take
up their own crosses. He "does not explain in the abstract the reasons
for suffering, but before all else He says: 'Follow me! Come! Take part
through your suffering in this work of saving the world, a salvation
achieved through my suffering! Through my cross! Gradually, *as the
individual takes up his cross*, spiritually uniting himself to the cross of

Christ, the salvific meaning of suffering is revealed before him." In other words, the individual discovers Christ himself as the personal answer to the problem of suffering. "He does not discover this meaning at his own human level, but at the level of the suffering of Christ." "At the same time," the Pope adds, "from this level of Christ the salvific meaning of suffering *descends to man's level* and becomes, in a sense, the individual's personal response. It is then that man finds in his suffering interior peace and even spiritual joy" (SD §26). For him, evil and suffering are not irreconcilable with God's goodness and power; rather they have become an indispensable element in God's providential plan.

Avery Dulles correctly states, "God's love is manifested in weakness and humiliation—in what John Paul II calls 'the omnipotence of humiliation on the Cross.' Christ triumphs over evil and enables us to share in his triumph, provided that we follow the path to which he calls us. The scandal of the cross thus becomes the key to the interpretation of the great mystery of suffering. The *mysterium pietatis*, which coincides with the mystery of redemption, is God's response to the *mysterium iniquitatis*."[23]

This interior process of conversion leads to the certainty that my suffering is not useless; indeed, it provides an irreplaceable service when united to the sufferings of Christ, because, like Christ, I am serving the salvation of others. "In the Body of Christ, which is ceaselessly born of the cross of the Redeemer, it is precisely suffering permeated by the spirit of Christ's sacrifice that is the *irreplaceable mediator and author of the good things* which are indispensable for the world's salvation. It is suffering more than anything else, which clears the way for the grace which transforms souls. Suffering, more than anything else, makes present in the history of humanity the powers of the Redemption. In that 'cosmic' struggle between the spiritual powers of good and evil,…human sufferings, united to the redemptive suffering of Christ, *constitute a special support for the powers of good*, and open the way to the victory of these salvific powers" (SD §27). In short, Christ wills to be united with those who suffer, and somehow he allows their sufferings to complete his own, to bring them to fruition. Of course there is no insufficiency in Christ's redemptive suffering; indeed, our 'making up' of what is 'lacking' derives its subjective redemptive efficacy from the infinite merits of Christ's cross and resurrection, his objective redemption.

The Good Samaritan

This evangelical theology of redemptive suffering gives rise to compassion for the suffering of others. "If God so loved us [in Christ], we also ought to love one another" (1 John 4:11). Indeed, having united our suffering with the sufferings of the crucified Christ, we are impelled to love of neighbor. "The parable of the Good Samaritan belongs to the Gospel of suffering. For it indicates what the relationship of each of us must be towards our suffering neighbor" (SD §28).

The Holy Father insists that Christ's revelation of the redemptive meaning of suffering should in no way be identified with passivity, docility, and resignation to human suffering. We have a basic obligation to stop human suffering that is a result of injustice. This obligation is fundamental to the morality of all cultures and civilizations. It bears witness to the fundamental moral values of Christian love of neighbor and human solidarity (SD §29). Yet there is more to this relationship to my neighbor than an obligation; we must also be internally disposed to be sensitive to the suffering of others—that is, compassionate. Says John Paul, "If Christ, who knows the interior of man, emphasizes this compassion, this means that it is important for our whole attitude toward others' suffering. Therefore, one must cultivate this sensitivity of heart, which bears witness to *compassion* towards a suffering person. Sometimes this compassion remains the only or principal expression of our love and solidarity with the sufferer" (SD §28). At the root of compassion is the Christian understanding that "man can fully discover his true self only in a sincere giving of himself." "A Good Samaritan is *the person capable of exactly such gift of self*" (SD §28).[24]

God sometimes permits suffering, then, as an opportunity "to release love, in order to give birth to works of love towards neighbor, in order to transform the whole of human civilization into a 'civilization of love.' In this love the salvific meaning of suffering is completely accomplished and reaches its definitive dimensions. Christ's words about the Final Judgment [Matt 25:34-45] enable us to understand this in all the simplicity and clarity of the Gospel" (SD §30). Every work of love toward one's neighbor, especially a suffering neighbor, is directed toward Christ himself. "These words about love, about actions of love, acts linked with human suffering, enable us once more to discover, at the basis of all *human sufferings, the same redemptive suffering of Christ.*

Christ said: 'You did it to me.' He Himself is the one who in each individual experiences love; He Himself is the one who receives help, when this is given to every suffering person, since His salvific suffering has been opened once and for all to every human suffering" (SD §30).

There remains to make the concluding point that in light of the Holy Father's theology of redemptive suffering the proper response to suffering is a double one. "At one and the same time Christ has taught man *to do good by his suffering and to do good to those who suffer.* In this double aspect He has completely revealed the meaning of suffering" (SD §30).

On the one hand, by suffering in loving union with the sufferings of the crucified Christ we apply through our suffering and our love the superabundant good, infinite in its merit and saving power, of the world's redemption accomplished through the suffering of Christ. It is in this way that one does good by one's suffering.

On the other hand, every work of love towards one's suffering neighbor is directed to Christ himself. "Assuredly, I say to you, inasmuch as you did it to one of the least of these My brethren, you did it to Me" (Matt 25:40): It is in this way that we do good to those who suffer.

Notes

1. Karol Wojtyla, *Sign of Contradiction*, 86.

2. Rogers, *Colossians*, 22.

3. In its *Decree on Justification*, the Council of Trent states: "even though 'Christ died for all' [2 Cor 5:15], still not all do receive the benefit of His death, but those only to whom the merit of His passion is imparted. Heinrich Denzinger, *Compendium of Creeds, Definitions, and Declarations on Matters of Faith and Morals*, §1523. According to Thomas Aquinas, Christ is "the propitiation for our sins, efficaciously for some, but sufficiently for all, because the price of his blood is sufficient for the salvation of all; but it has its effect only in the elect" (*Commentary on Titus* 1:2:6; idem, *Summa theologiae* III. 48.2).

4. I am grateful to Marsha Williamson for pressing me to be clear on this difference.

5. Yes, this is a version of Catholic synergism, in which man's free response participates in God's gift of salvation, but it is neither pelagian nor semi-pelagian. See my book, *Divine Election: A Catholic Orientation in Dogmatic and Ecumenical Perspective*.

6. Schaeffer, *True Spirituality*, 83.

7. Calvin, *Calvin's Commentaries to the Galatians, Ephesians...*, 319.

8. Grisez, *The Way of the Lord Jesus*, Vol. 2, *Living a Christian Life*, 33.

9. Schaeffer, *The Finished Work of Christ: The Truth of Romans 1-8*, 176.

10. On this, see Hans Urs von Balthasar, "Bought at a Great Price," 81.

11. I am grateful to my colleague, Peter Williamson, holder of the Cardinal Maida Chair in Biblical Studies, Sacred Heart Major Seminary, for sharing this point with me. He added: "Here are some references where [a form of *paschō* (noun pl, *pathēmata*)] is found: Luke 24:26, 46; Acts 3:18; 17:3; 26:23; Rom 8:17; 2 Cor 1:5; Phil 1:29; 3:10; 1 Thess 2:14; 2 Tim 2:3; 1 Pet 1:11; 2:21; 3:18; 4:1; 5:1, 10. I never found *thlipsis* in that context" (personal email, 8/28/17).

12. Schweizer, *The Letter to the Colossians: A Commentary*, 101, 104-5.

13. Moule, *The Cambridge Greek Testament Commentary*, 76-77.

14. Gundry, *Commentary on the New Testament*, 801.

15. Ashley, *Choosing a World-View*, 319.

16. (SD §24) The Holy Father continues explaining: "Only within this radius and dimension of the Church as the Body of Christ, which continually develops in space and time, can one think and speak of 'what is lacking' in the sufferings of Christ. The Apostle, in fact, makes this clear when he writes of 'completing what is lacking in Christ's afflictions for the sake of his body, that is the Church.' It is precisely *the Church*, which ceaselessly draws on the infinite resources of the Redemption, introducing it into the life of humanity, *which is the dimension* in which the redemptive suffering of Christ can be constantly completed by the suffering of man" (SD §24). That Christ's sufferings are inexhaustible and infinite in their merit and saving power is also expressed in the following passage: "And so the Church sees in all Christ's suffering brothers and sisters as it were a *multiple subject of His supernatural power*...The Gospel of suffering is being written unceasingly, and it speaks unceasingly with the words of this strange paradox: the springs of divine power gush forth precisely in the midst of human weakness. Those who share in the sufferings of Christ preserve in their own sufferings a very special *particle of the infinite treasure* of the world's Redemption, and can share this treasure with others" (SD §27).

17. Hans Urs von Balthasar, *You Crown the Year with Your Goodness*, 30.

18. *CoC*, II: "[The] truth of our faith does not exclude but demands the participation of each and every human being in Christ's sacrifice in collaboration with the Redeemer. As we said above, no human being could carry out the work of redemption by offering a substitutive sacrifice 'for the sins of the whole world' (cf. 1 John 2:2). But it is also true that each one is called upon to participate in Christ's sacrifice and to collaborate with him in the work of redemption carried out by him. The Apostle Paul says so explicitly when he writes to the Colossians: 'Now I rejoice in my sufferings for your sake, and in my flesh I complete what is lacking in Christ's afflictions for the sake of his body, that is, the Church' (Col 1:24)...Here we have one of the cornerstones of the specific Christian spirituality that we are called upon to reactivate in our life by virtue of Baptism itself which,

as St. Paul says (cf. Rom 6:3-4) brings about sacramentally our death and burial by immersing us in Christ's salvific sacrifice. If Christ has redeemed humanity by accepting the cross and death 'for all', the solidarity of Christ with every human being contains in itself the call to cooperate in solidarity with him in the work of redemption. This is the eloquence of the Gospel. This is especially the eloquence of the cross. This is the importance of Baptism, which, as we shall see in due course, already effects in itself the participation of every person in the salvific work, in which he is associated with Christ by the same divine vocation" (447-49).

19. Cited in Saward, *Christ is the Answer*, 88. Saward states the Holy Father's view precisely: "To suffer in loving union with Christ is to be an apostle, a missionary, an active laborer in the vineyard of the Lord."

20. Bryce, "Does Suffering Lack Meaning? " 437.

21. Hildebrand, *Transformation in Christ*, 370.

22. Ashley, *Choosing a World-View*, 308.

23. Dulles, *The Splendor of Faith*, 92.

24. As the Holy Father explains, "Following the parable of the Gospel, we could say that suffering, which is present under so many different forms in our human world, is also present in order to *unleash love in the human person*, that unselfish gift of one's 'I' on behalf of other people, especially those who suffer. The world of human suffering unceasingly calls for, so to speak, another world: the world of human love; and in a certain sense man owes to suffering that unselfish love which stirs in his heart and actions" (SD §29).

Penelope Grace Deely
2014–2016

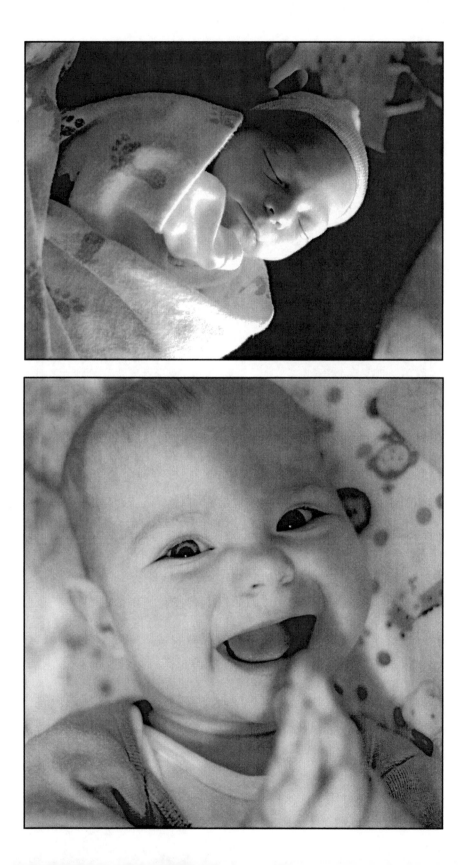

CHAPTER 5

Baptized into Christ's Death

True spirituality cannot be abstracted from truth at one end nor from the whole man and the whole culture at the other. If there is a true spirituality, it must encompass all.[1]

Death, as a movement that leaves its mark on human existence, must not be regarded by man himself as something merely biological or external but, rather, must be assimilated spiritually and humanly so as to come to the fruition that this event can and should have in us. This means, therefore, that for the human being everything depends on correctly grasping the dying movement in his life, starting from the little humiliation and onward to major failures (of health, of physical or mental abilities: *the death of loved ones is a part of a person's own death*, and so on).[2]

Not only do we only know God through Jesus Christ, but we only know ourselves through Jesus Christ; we only know life and death through Jesus Christ. Apart from Jesus Christ we cannot know the meaning of our life or of our death, of God, or of ourselves.[3]

In this book, I have given an answer to the question about the meaning of suffering, evil, and death from a Christian faith perspective. As Ratzinger urges in the middle epigraph above, I have tried to grasp correctly the dying movement in man's life. This is because a true spirituality of the meaning of suffering, evil, and death must be grounded in the truth. "Christ called himself Truth, not custom."[4] Hence, I have responded to the claim that the Bible is not a reliable source of knowledge.

I have also sketched some arguments showing that the existence of evil and suffering are not inconsistent with belief in a God who is sovereign in goodness, power, and knowledge. I have argued that there is a limit to such arguments and, therefore, that there is no answer to the question of the meaning of suffering and evil without the crucified God, the Incarnate Word, Jesus Christ, and his resurrection. In the immediately preceding chapter, I have developed the notion of redemptive suffering so as to argue that "Christ gives the answer to the question about suffering and the meaning of suffering not only by His teaching,... but most of all by His own suffering" (SD §18).

In particular, when we are experiencing the uselessness of suffering, a transformation is possible when we are taught how to suffer. Indeed, according to John Paul II, "A source of joy is found in the *overcoming of the sense of the uselessness of suffering...* . The discovery of the salvific meaning of suffering in union with Christ *transforms* this depressing *feeling*" (SD §27). I urge the readers who have followed me up to this point to ask for the gift of faith that comes only through Christ so that they might experience the meaning of suffering by allowing their sufferings to share in the sufferings of Christ and hence be a consolation to themselves and others (cf. 2 Cor 1:3-12).

Now, this concluding chapter is particularly written for those readers who have sometimes found hard going the terrain covered in the previous chapters of this book. I return to the concerns of the late Paul Kalanithi, a neurosurgeon who died in March 2015. I discussed his struggle with the meaning of death in the first chapter. I will respond to him again in this concluding chapter by presenting three interpretations of death, namely, the idealist, materialist, and Christian understanding of death.[5]

The Denial of Death?

Each person has the certitude that he must die because of his finitude and mortality. He comes to this certitude in different ways. "Police officers are reminded of human mortality every time they are called to a fatal crash. Death is a routine part of life in our major hospitals. And at some point, the personal reality of death hits home. Death does not just happen to other people. It is going to happen to me."[6] At my beloved Penelope's Funeral Mass this certitude was reconfirmed for me. But I especially thought of all the people present who were being confronted at this mass with their mortality and, also, with the fragility of their existence, particularly given that this was a mass for the sudden and completely unexpected death of a young child. It is impossible to deny the reality of death—but how long would the intimations of mortality and fragility last?

I thought to myself: would the people here at the funeral consider that they exist, "not only as a being conditioned by the reality of death, but also as a being able to think about this fact, and to live authentically (or not) in the face of death"?[7] Death is unavoidable. It is the abyss. Would they think about this fact after the funeral? Would they distract themselves from death? And would they think about how to live authentically in its face? The great seventeenth-century French philosopher, scientist, and mathematician, Blaise Pascal (1623-1662), wrote, "Being unable to cure death, wretchedness and ignorance, men have decided, in order to be happy, not to think about such things."[8] They adopt the strategy of *diversion*, according to Pascal. They desperately avoid thinking about death and about all the issues it raises. Says Thomas V. Morris, "We try to do everything we can to create within us a sense that death is not near, that it can be ignored, that ultimate issues are mists far beyond the horizon."[9]

Now, to live authentically in the face of death requires us to reflect on the big issues of life so as to do what is needed to live a good life in preparing for a good death. If we are diverted by other matters, never grappling with the big issues of life, in particular, the question regarding the meaning of death, says Pascal, "We run heedlessly into the abyss after putting something in front of us to stop us seeing it."[10]

Minimally, therefore, to live authentically in the face of death requires that we must not be distracted by other issues. We must look at death in the face. In the words of the *Catechism of the Catholic Church*, "Death is the end of earthly life. Our lives are measured by time, in the course of which we change, grow old and, as with all living beings on earth, death seems like the normal end of life. That aspect of death lends urgency to our lives: remembering our mortality helps us to realize that we have only a limited time in which to bring our lives to fulfillment" (§1007).

In addition, for a man to live authentically as a "being towards death" (Heidegger[11]) requires one to regard death itself as something that is not "merely biological or external but, rather," as Ratzinger states in the epigraph to this chapter, "must be assimilated spiritually and humanly so as to come to the fruition that this event can and should have in us" (OTD, 250). To live authentically in the face of death requires dealing with hope—and even expectation—the anxiety of death that we all experience. How do we overcome covering up with resignation and gloom this anxiety when facing the fact of the reality of our eventual death? Are there points of contact with human experience that would open one up to understanding death from a Christian faith perspective? The Second Vatican Council puts this perspective in this way:

> It is in the face of death that the riddle [of] human existence grows most acute. Not only is man tormented by pain and by the advancing deterioration of his body, but even more so by a dread of perpetual extinction. He rightly follows the intuition of his heart when he abhors and repudiates the utter ruin and total disappearance of his own person. He rebels against death because he bears in himself an eternal seed which cannot be reduced to sheer matter. All the endeavors of technology, though useful in the extreme, cannot calm his anxiety; for prolongation of biological life is unable to satisfy that desire for higher life which is inescapably lodged in his breast. Although the mystery of death utterly beggars the imagination, the Church has been taught by divine revelation and firmly teaches that man has been created by God for a blissful purpose beyond the reach of earthly misery. In addition, that bodily death from which man would have been immune had he not sinned (cf. Wis 1:13; 2:23-24; Rom 5:21; 6:23; Jas 1:15) will be vanquished, according to the Christian faith, when man who was ruined by his own doing is restored to wholeness by an almighty and merciful Savior. For God has called man and still calls him so that with his entire

being he might be joined to Him in an endless sharing of a divine life beyond all corruption. Christ won this victory when He rose to life, for by His death He freed man from death. Hence to every thoughtful man a solidly established faith provides the answer to his anxiety about what the future holds for him. At the same time faith gives him the power to be united in Christ with his loved ones who have already been snatched away by death; faith arouses the hope that they have found true life with God. (GS §18)

In this passage, we find all the essential elements of the Christian perspective on death. Several key points stand out. Making sense of the meaning of life is a particularly perplexing task in the face of death. Among several factors having to do with growing old, one stands out in particular, namely, the dread that death is the end not only of earthly life, but the extinction of my existence as such. Still, man's deep-seated intuition drives him to "abhor and repudiate the utter ruin and total disappearance of his own person." Is this intuition trustworthy? In other words, is there any good reason to believe in personal immortality, in life after death, rather than in final annihilation?[12]

I think we can say that Jesus' resurrection appearances in the biblical testimony provide us "with firsthand knowledge of what lies beyond death," giving us "a well-founded answer to that question."[13] But rather than develop here an argument for the historicity of the resurrection, or even repeat my argument set out in Chapter 1 about testimonial knowledge, I shall take another approach to answering that question. I shall highlight one of many arguments supporting man's rebellion against death because "he bears in himself an eternal seed which cannot be reduced to sheer matter."

Major premise:	If life ends in final annihilation, then life does not have an end worth living for.
Minor premise:	Life must have an end worth living for.
Conclusion:	Therefore life does not end in final annihilation.

Explanation of the major premise: If "the whole temple of man's achievements is destined to be buried beneath the debris of a universe in ruins," and "no thought, no heroism can sustain an individual life beyond the grave," then we must build our lives on what Bertrand Russell calls "the firm foundation of unyielding despair."[14] But this is psychologically impossible and logically contradictory; despair is not a "firm foundation" but precisely the lack of one.[15]

The brief reference to Bertrand Russell's claims raises the question, "How, in such an alien and inhuman world, can so powerless a creature as man preserve his aspirations untarnished? A strange mystery it is that nature, omnipotent but blind, in the revolutions of her secular hurryings through the abysses of space, has brought forth at last a child, subject still to her power, but gifted with sight, with knowledge of good and evil, with the capacity of judging all the works of his unthinking mother [nature]."[16] In this context, I want especially to criticize Russell's claim, which is the claim of the naturalist—nature is all there is, there is no God, and man is just a part of nature—whose view of reality reflects a materialist anthropology in which man is merely the chance product of matter in motion. In short, man lives in an *impersonal* universe, according to the materialist, and hence personality is not intrinsic to existence. But then how does one explain man's personality from the impersonal beginning, plus time, plus chance?

Francis Schaeffer presents the materialist with the following disjunctive syllogism: "Either there is a personal beginning to everything, or one has what the impersonal throws up by chance out of the time sequence" (GWT, 114). The question is whether reality, especially human beings, finds its origin in the impersonal, plus time, plus chance? If the world should turn out to be the chance product of matter-in-motion, doesn't that mean that "those things that make him man—hope of purpose and significance, love, notions of morality and rationality, beauty and verbal communication—would be absurd, indeed, ultimately unfulfillable and thus meaningless," i.e., irrational? (GWT, 116). In other words, isn't materialism irrational? Schaeffer argues that it is, and he thinks this conclusion is logically inescapable. He says, "No one has presented an idea, let alone demonstrated it to be feasible, to explain how the impersonal beginning, plus time, plus chance, can give personality. We are distracted by a flourish of endless words, and lo, personality has appeared out of the hat!" Adds Schaeffer, "As a result, either the thinker must say man is dead, because personality is a mirage; or else he must hang his reason on a hook outside the door and cross the threshold into the leap of faith which is the new level of despair" (GWT, 115).

In sum, the materialist is left with an unhappy dilemma: either nihilism or fideism. Whichever he chooses, he must face the practical fear of the *impersonal* (the universe is ultimately mere mass and energy, and hence remains silent), of *nonbeing* (of not knowing who I am and whether I have a valid, meaningful existence), and of *death* (with our hope being only in this life, it is doubtful whether life has any objective meaning or purpose at all).[18]

In contrast, the Christian affirms the truth that there is a personal beginning to everything—the personal-infinite God who is there. As Joseph Ratzinger wrote, "The principle that represents the fundamental conviction of Christian faith and of its philosophy remains true: '*In principio erat Verbum*'—at the beginning of all things stands the creative power of reason. Now as then, Christian faith represents the choice in favor of the priority of reason and of rationality . . . Even today, by reason of its choosing to assert the primacy of reason, Christianity remains 'enlightened', and I think," adds Ratzinger, "that any enlightenment that cancels this choice [see disjunctive syllogism above] must, contrary to all appearances, mean, not an evolution, but an involution, a shrinking, of enlightenment."[19] Schaeffer thought he had found the Achilles heel of materialism—Ratzinger agrees, and so do I.

Schaeffer was persuaded that, not only did the serious Christian have nothing to fear intellectually from materialistic critics, but also that the Christian answer to the source and meaning of human personality "should make us overwhelmingly excited." "But more than this," Schaeffer adds, "we are returned to a personal relationship with the God who is there." Thus, he writes, in a paragraph that summarizes his most basic convictions:

> If we are unexcited Christians, we should go back and
> see what is wrong [with our thinking]. We are sur-
> rounded by a generation that can find 'no one home'
> in the universe. If anything marks our generation, it
> is this. In contrast to this, as a Christian I know who I
> am; and I know the personal God who is there. I speak,
> and he hears. I am not surrounded by mere mass, or
> only energy particles [as Bertrand Russell confessed],
> but he is there (and he is not silent). And if I have ac-

cepted Christ as my Savior, then though it will not be perfect in this life, yet moment-by-moment, on the basis of the finished work of Christ, this person-to person relationship with the God who is there can have reality to me (GWT, 190).

Furthermore, the issue is about personal immortality, namely, that *I* survive my death from this earthly life. Hence, being kept biologically alive is not sufficient. In this light, we can understand the point that *Gaudium et Spes* makes: "All the endeavors of technology, though useful in the extreme, cannot calm his anxiety [about death and final annihilation]; for prolongation of biological life is unable to satisfy that desire for higher life which is inescapably lodged in his breast." Yes, death is a biological event, a bodily failure, but the bodily aspect of death—notwithstanding the protests of the materialist—is only one aspect of that event, and not the only thing that is at stake here (OTD, 246).

Moreover, the Christian faith holds that "death entered the world on account of man's sin."[20] The *Catechism of the Catholic Church* explains, "Even though man's nature is mortal, God had destined him not die. Death was therefore contrary to the plans of God the Creator, and entered the world as a consequence of Sin. 'Bodily death, from which man would have been immune had he not sinned' is thus 'the last enemy' of man left to be conquered" (§1008). Hence, the Christian faith perspective offers us an understanding of death in which death is transformed from within such that it, says Ratzinger, "has acquired a new significance in Christ and in terms of Christ" (OTD, 250). He adds, "Christ won this victory [over death] when He rose to life, for by His death He freed man from death." I will return to the significance of this perspective below. For now, let us briefly consider two non-Christian interpretations of death.

Interpretations of Death

The first interpretation of death that has a hold on many people in our culture is the materialistic explanation.[21] I considered this explanation in the first chapter in our brief discussion of Paul Kalanithi's struggle with dying. I have also examined it in the last section. Although Kalanithi was a man of science who studied biology and neuroscience, he never really accepted the idea that science could explain everything. He did consider the possibility of a material conception of reality, namely, that impersonal matter is ultimately all there is, that immaterial realities, such as souls and God are outmoded concepts, that man is simply the chance product of matter in motion.

Eventually Kalanithi came to see that "to make science the arbiter of metaphysics [of what is ultimately real] is to banish not only God from the world but also love, hate, meaning—to consider a world that is self-evidently *not* the world we live in."[22] But the basic reality of human life stands compellingly against a material conception of reality, against the idea that man is just the chance product of matter in motion. So, in this light, Kalanithi "returned to the central values of Christianity—sacrifice, redemption, forgiveness—because I found them so compelling."[23]

The problem with Kalanithi's position is that it appears to operate with an "absolute dichotomy between reason and non-reason." In other words, explains Schaeffer, "that which would give meaning is always separated from reason, reason only leads to knowledge" in the sense of the materialistic explanation. "So," continues Schaeffer, "rationality, including modern science, will lead only to pessimism. Man is only the machine, man is only the zero, and nothing has any real meaning. I am nothing... . I have no meaning; I die; man is dead."[24] Of course Kalanithi rejects the position that man is nothing. I discussed this in the first chapter, so I will not return to it now.

What I will say, however, is that the problem with Kalanithi's acceptance of these Christian values, the ones he found so compelling, is that he could not say anything definitive or certain about God. God is there and he is not silent—or is He, according to Kalanithi?[25] Indeed, it appears for him that God is silent since he holds that it is impossible to credit "revelation with any epistemic authority." In other words, divine revelation, in short, the Scriptures, are not a trustworthy source of knowledge and hence one would not be rational in holding its claims to be true, according to Kalanithi.[26] Thus, he had no credible response to the materialist conception of reality and death.

This explanation presupposes that man is just the chance product of matter in motion; he is just a material thing, and hence man is ultimately surrounded by impersonal matter and energy. Thus, this interpretation rules out an immaterial principle, a soul, and personal immortality. Mental states, on this view, are just brain states. Accordingly, this view "maintains that in death an organism ceases to be, just as it once began to be" (OTD, 247). On this view, our hope is only in this life. It leaves us with two possibilities. One, explains Ratzinger, from the response to the challenge of death "in the face of nothingness," we are thrown back upon ourselves, "now in a final act of responsibility to fill this meaningless structure of life with the most sublime meaning by our own power," and two, we are "down to that other philistine existentialism that is formulated in terms that were already quoted in the Bible: 'Let us eat and drink, for tomorrow we die!' (1 Cor 15:32; cf. Is 22:13)."

In my judgment, materialism does not help us to deal with the anxiety that when all is said and done, life is meaningless, pointless, and utterly futile. Does our life have meaning? The Christian perspective responds to this question with the knowledge that our life has meaning only if our death also has meaning, and our death can only have meaning in the light of the cross and resurrection of Jesus Christ. "Because of Christ, Christian death has a positive meaning" (CCC §1010).

The second interpretation of death that also has a hold on many in our culture is the one that I will call, following Ratzinger, the "idealistic" interpretation. This view assumes that reality consists of hierarchical levels—upstairs and downstairs—in which the entire world of material is the lower level, being less important than the higher level of spiritual existence. Man, therefore, consists of two parts: material being, the body, and immaterial reality, the soul, which are united in one single nature. On this view, death is a friend, as it were; indeed, there is redemption in death, because at death the soul, the spiritual dimension of human nature, is freed from its dependency on the body. Ratzinger explains:

> According to the . . . hierarchy of being, the material component, the body, as a matter of principle can be only a de-authentication of what is truly human, that is, of the spiritual component. Dying, then, is simply being set free for what is authentic; it is liberation and redemption. Consequently, death is the "friend" who frees man from the imprisonment of the body and purchases his entrance into his authentic existence, the im-

mortal, purely spiritual, and eternal being of the soul (OTD, 245).

There are several objections to make against this idealistic interpretation of death. First, it is not justified in claiming that the body deauthenticates what is truly human. God created the material reality a good thing, and hence the body cannot be considered a prison of the soul because the body itself is good. Furthermore, this view suggests that the body is like a suit of clothes that man can take off and still be fully himself, as if the body is just an appendage and not essential to man's humanity. No, body and soul are essential to our humanity, to the full person as a totality.[27]

In the Christian view of man, on the contrary, man is "a living union of spirit and body, embodied spirit and spiritually formed body, the two so united that one without the other would no longer be a human being at all, who is one precisely in the other." Adds Ratzinger, "Man is 'authentic,' is himself, precisely in the body; being human means 'being in the body'; corporeality is the authenticity of man" (OTD, 245). Hence, we cannot properly think about death unless we see that death is "precisely an attack on the authenticity of man as well, which shatters the instrument of the spirit along with the body and suddenly interrupts this entity that has scarcely begun" (OTD, 246).

The Christian faith perspective affirms personal immortality and hence that the spiritual soul can survive the loss of the body. But without my body I am not fully myself, and so I am incomplete, and "not the whole human being."[28] That is why the Christian faith affirms not only that "the human *body* shares in the dignity of 'the image of God'" (CCC §364), but also the redemption of the body. "The Resurrection of Christ effects for us the resurrection of our bodies. . . . His Resurrection was, as it were, an instrument for the accomplishment of our resurrection. It may also be called the model of ours, inasmuch as His Resurrection was the most perfect of all. And as His body, rising to immortal glory, was changed, so shall our bodies also, before frail and mortal, be restored and clothed with glory and immortality. In the language of the Apostle: We look for the Savior, our Lord Jesus Christ, who will reform the body of our lowness, made like to the body of his glory."[29] That is why the whole man is redeemed and hence receives a resurrected body. Says Thomas Joseph White, "Consequently, even if we affirm the existence of the soul that continues to subsist after death (as the Catholic Church teaches), we also need to affirm the resurrection of the body in order to make sense of the future destiny of the whole human person, body and soul."[30] And it is precisely the perspective of the whole human person, the full person as a totality, that is missing from the idealist interpretation of death.

St. Paul writes, "But someone will ask, 'How are the dead raised? With what kind of body do they come?'" (1 Cor 15:35). As the *Catechism of the Catholic Church* states, "It is very commonly accepted that the life of the human person continues in a spiritual fashion after death. [This is the idealist interpretation of death.] But how can we believe that the body, so clearly mortal, could rise to everlasting life?" (§996) Of course, since the Bible affirms that the whole human person—soul and body—will be in the Lord's presence, I have wondered what my beloved granddaughter Penny will look like as she was only 2½ years old when she died and, as a baptized innocent, went to be with the Lord. St. Augustine of Hippo (354-430) addresses this question in his *magnum opus*, *The City of God.* He states:

> What, then, are we to say of infants [or toddlers], if not that they will not rise in that diminutive body in which they died, but shall receive by the marvelous and rapid operation of God that body which time by a slower process would have given them? For in the Lord's words, where He says, "Not a hair of your head shall perish" [Luke 21:18], it is asserted that nothing which was possessed shall be wanting; but it is not said that nothing which was not possessed shall be given. To the dead infant [or toddler] there was wanting the perfect stature of its body; for even the perfect infant [or toddler] lacks the perfection of bodily size, being capable of further growth. This perfect stature is, in a sense, so possessed by all that they are conceived and born with it,—that is, they have it potentially, though not yet in actual bulk; just as all the members of the body are potentially in the seed, though, even after the child is born, some of them, the teeth for example, may be wanting. In this seminal principle of every substance, there seems

to be, as it were, the beginning of everything which does not yet exist, or rather does not appear, but which in process of time will come into being, or rather into sight. In this, therefore, the child who is to be tall or short is already tall or short. And in the resurrection of the body, we need, for the same reason, fear no bodily loss; for though all should be of equal size, and reach gigantic proportions, lest the men who were largest here should lose anything of their bulk and it should perish, in contradiction to the words of Christ, who said that not a hair of their head should perish, yet why should there lack the means by which that wonderful Worker should make such additions, seeing that He is the Creator, who Himself created all things out of nothing?[31]

In other words, everything that Penny potentially possessed in her being, her nature, her size, her hair color, shape of her face, her appearance, and so forth, would be realized in the resurrection of her body. God the Creator, does not lack the power to bring her reality into its fullness, that is, to rise in that body that she would have had had she grown up. We walk by faith and not by sight here (2 Cor 5:7). Hence, we are not permitted to wade any further into these deep waters. *I Can Only Imagine*, a popular Christian song, envisions our face-to-face, side-by-side encounter with our Creator.[32]

A second objection to make against this idealistic view is that the experience of death is not taken seriously. Death is experienced as an enemy and not a friend. Consider Jesus' agony in the Garden of Gethsemane (Matt 26: 36-46; Luke 22:38-46). Jesus begins "to tremble and be distressed," writes Mark (14:33). "My soul is troubled, even to death" (14:34). Death is an enemy in the Christian scheme of things, indeed, death is a consequence of sin, but it is the last enemy to be destroyed (1 Cor 15:26); it is swallowed up in Christ's victory (1 Cor 15:54f.). In this light we can understand why "*Death is transformed by Christ.* Jesus, the Son of God, also himself suffered the death that is part of the human condition. Yet, despite his anguish as he faced death, he accepted it in an act of complete and free submission to his Father's will. The obedience of Jesus has transformed the curse of death into a blessing" (CCC §1009).[33]

A third objection to make against this idealistic view is that it fails to understand the relationship between the soul and bodily processes. Materialism is wrong to think that the only thing at stake in death is the bodily processes. But the idealistic view does not see that "It is not the soul's departure that makes it impossible for the body to work; rather, the failure of the body itself puts an end to life" (OTD, 246). In the celebrated *Star Trek* series there is a race of extraterrestrial humanoid warrior species called Klingons. The body of a dead warrior is viewed mainly as an empty shell, and that is because the soul has left the body. But this loses sight of the fact that it is the body's failure to service the soul that results in the death of the person. "On a broken instrument, the soul can no longer play" (OTD, 247). Ratzinger quotes a Catholic physician on this matter: "'Medicine sees in death a bodily failure.... One does not die because the soul leaves the body. One dies because the necessary conditions for bodily life are no longer present. The body leaves the soul and sets it free'" (OTD, 246). It is time now to turn back to the Christian interpretation of death.

"We Were Baptized Into Christ's Death"

In light of the Christian understanding of death, I will briefly consider the loss of a loved one. Ratzinger is right, as he says in the epigraph to this chapter, "for the human being everything depends on correctly grasping the dying movement in his life, starting from the little humiliation and onward to major failures (of health, of physical or mental abilities: *the death of loved ones is a part of a person's own death*, and so on)." Even there, in the great mystery that is death, God is to be found and hence "In oceans deep My faith will stand." This is the Christian gist of the meaning of the verses of the Hillsong United song, "Oceans (Where Feet May Fail)." The verses of that song teach us about how to suffer in and with Christ, the one who will keep my eyes above the waves, so that in oceans deep my faith will stand. How so? The song continues:

> Your grace abounds in deepest waters,
> Your sovereign hand
> Will be my guide
> Where feet may fail and fear surrounds me
> My soul will rest in Your embrace

Spirit lead me where my trust is without borders
Let me walk upon the waters
Wherever You would call me
Take me deeper than my feet could ever wander
And my faith will be made stronger
In the presence of my Savior.

How, then, do we give spiritual meaning to the dying process? How does God's grace abound in the deepest waters of that mystery that is death, with his sovereign hand being my guide, especially here where feet may fail and fear surrounds me? St. Paul's answer to this question is this: "We were baptized into [Christ's] death" (Rom 6:3). Baptism into the death of Christ means participating in his death on the cross and hence his resurrection. How, then, do we understand dying and rising with Christ? This is a New Testament promise that expresses the basis of Christian hope, keeping man from discouragement (CCC §1818): "The saying is trustworthy, for if we have died with him, we will also live with him" (2 Tim 2:11). A brief explanation is in order as I conclude.

In Chapter 3, I explained the Christian faith perspective that man would have been immune to bodily death had he not originally sinned (cf. Wis 1:13, 2:23-24; Rom 5:21, 6:23; Jas 1:15). In this light, this perspective also holds—we stated in Chapter 4—that central to the authentic acceptance of death man "must accept [death] as a breaking-off of his self-assertiveness and as the development of a new freedom of spirit and of body and thereby transform its meaning or, more precisely, make the already existing transformation of meaning fruitful in his life." Ratzinger continues: "In this way the dying movement, instead of being a blind fate, can become a very practical sort of training in true freedom and can become the process through which someone becomes a 'new man'—which means precisely a Christian" (OTD, 250-51). This practical training takes place in light of the perspective that death is vanquished by the death and resurrection of an almighty and merciful Savior who restores man to wholeness by calling him to an endless sharing of divine life beyond all corruption.

Ratzinger, consequently, urges us to see in dying more than the conclusion of our biological existence. Rather, we should accept and spiritually rework the dying process in light of its being transformed by way of the "acceptance and spiritual assimilation of [our] baptism" (OTD,

251). What is baptism all about? Here is the answer of St. Paul: "Do you not know that all of us who have been baptized into Christ Jesus were baptized into his death? We were buried therefore with him by baptism into death, in order that, just as Christ was raised from the dead by the glory of the Father, we too might walk in newness of life" (Rom 6:3-4).

So, in baptism we unite our dying movement that marks our life as a whole with Christ's death and resurrection. Through Christ's death on the cross, death itself underwent a fundamental transformation in meaning. "O death, where is your victory? O death, where is your sting?" St. Paul's answer: "Thanks be to God, who gives us the victory through our Lord Jesus Christ" (1 Cor 15:55, 57).

In this light, we must understand that the sacrament of baptism incorporates the one baptized with Christ, his death, and his resurrection. As Ratzinger put it, "Baptism is participation in Christ's death and Resurrection, dying with Christ and thus gaining a share in the Resurrection as the necessary fruit of death" (OTD, 251) From the moment of our sacramental dying with Christ in baptism, adds Ratzinger, "it is an anticipation of a real death: all of our dying, which marks and permeates our whole life as the constant *processus mortis in vitam* [advance of death into life], is now no longer merely our own dying but, rather, is because of baptism and for the sake of baptism an act of divine grace."

The gradual outpouring of the grace of baptism comes to fulfillment in our definitive bodily death. In other words, concludes Ratzinger, "The whole process of dying is, if we accept it in faith, the realization of our being baptized, which comes to an end only on our deathbed: it is being overshadowed by the Cross of Christ and, thus, by the life of Christ" (ibid.).

This last point enables us to see that baptism into the death of Christ, as also resurrection with him in baptism, provides us with a "marvelous reversal" of the meaning of baptism, for this "frightful negation of the whole man," as it were, "now becomes the prerequisite for a new positive reality: out of destruction is born the new thing" (OTD, 252). This is a particularly important answer for me. I have attempted in this book to provide a context for understanding the meaning of Penny's death. "Hence to every thoughtful man a solidly established faith provides the answer to his anxiety about what the future holds for him." This is the perspective that I have shared with others: "At the same time faith gives him the power to be united in Christ with his loved ones who have already been snatched away by death; faith [in Christ's resurrection] arouses the hope that they have found true life with God" (GS §18). This was and remains my hope for my beloved granddaughter Penelope.

As I wrote in the Introduction to this book, I have the consolation that Penny is at peace because she was a baptized innocent and hence is in the presence of the Lord, seeing the face of God. What also brings consolation is the well-grounded hope that by God's merciful grace when I stand before him I will hear him say to me (adapting Luc Ferry[34]), "Come quickly, your granddaughter Penelope eagerly awaits you." I end my book thinking of Johnny Cash's musical rendition of First Corinthians 15:55 that death is neither a victory nor even a wound; hope springs eternal due to my redeemer.[35]

Notes

1. Schaeffer, *The God Who is There*, 144. See, idem, *True Spirituality*.

2. Ratzinger, *Dogma and Preaching, Applying Christian Doctrine to Daily Life*, "On the Theology of Death," [hereafter 'OTD'] 243-54, and at 250; emphasis added. For Ratzinger's theological treatise developing his theology of death, see *Eschatology, Death and Eternal Life*.

3. Pascal, *Pensées*, no. 182. Cited in Thomas V. Morris, *Making Sense of It All, Pascal and the Meaning of Life*, 28.

4. Tertullian, "On the Veiling of Virgins," Chapter 1, "Truth Rather to be Appealed to than Custom, and Truth Progressive in its Development."

5. I am particularly indebted to Ratzinger's essay, "On the Theology of Death" for my reflections in this concluding chapter. Also helpful is Ferry, *A Brief History of Thought, A Philosophical Guide to Living*, 261-64.

6. McGrath, *Intellectuals Don't Need God & Other Modern Myths*, 44.

7. White, *The Light of Christ, An Introduction to Catholicism*, 261.

8. Pascal, *Pensées*, no. 133. Cited in Morris, *Making Sense of It All*, 31.

9. Morris, *Making Sense of It All*, 35.

10. Pascal, *Pensées*, #166, as cited in Morris, *Making Sense of It All*, 34.

11. Heidegger, *Being and Time*, Section 51, 233-245.

12. There are many arguments supporting the claim for life after death. See for a sketch of these arguments, Kreeft and Tacelli, 237-70.

13. Ratzinger, "Faith, Philosophy and Theology," 23.

14. Russell, "A Free Man's Worship," in *The Meaning of Life*, 56.

15. Kreeft and Tacelli, *Handbook of Catholic Apologetics*, 262.

16. Russell, "A Free Man's Worship," 56.

17. The next few paragraphs contain material drawn from my article, "The Christian faith as a way of life: in appreciation of Francis Schaeffer (on the fiftieth anniversary of L'Abri Fellowship)," 241-52.

18. Schaeffer, *True Spirituality*, 123-24.

19. Ratzinger, *Truth and Tolerance*, 181.

20. I discussed this effect of original sin in Chapter 3.

21. For a brief refutation of materialism, see Kreeft and Tacelli, 240-47.

22. Kalanithi, *When Breath Becomes Air*, 169.

23. Ibid., 171.

24. Schaeffer, *He Is There and He Is Not Silent*, 54-55.

25. Schaeffer answers this question persuasively in his book, *He Is There and He Is Not Silent*.

26. I dealt with Kalanithi's claim in Chapter 1.

27. This, too, is the view of John Paul II in his *magnum opus*, *Man and Woman He Created Them: A Theology of the Body*. It is also the view of Reformed philosopher, Herman Dooyeweerd, *Reformation and Scholasticism in Philosophy*, Volume Three, Chapters 1-3.

28. Thomas Aquinas, Commentary on St. Paul's First Letter to the Corinthians 15:17-19, *Super Epistolam Pauli Apostoli*, Passage 19, as cited in *Aquinas, Selected Philosophical Writings*, Translated and edited by Timothy McDermott (New York: Oxford University Press, 1993), 192-93.

29. *Catechism of the Council of Trent*, Article V, Part II, "The Third Day He Rose from the Dead," §63.

30. White, *The Light of Christ, An Introduction to Catholicism*, 263.

31. St. Augustine, *The City of God*, Book XXII, Chapter 14.—Whether Infants Shall Rise in that Body Which They Would Have Had Had They Grown Up.

32. https://en.wikipedia.org/wiki/I_Can_Only_Imagine_(MercyMe_song).

33. Ratzinger writes in a similar vein, "Christ does not die in the noble detachment of the philosopher [such as in the death of Socrates]. He dies in tears. On his lips was the bitter taste of abandonment and isolation in all its horror. Here the hubris that would be the equal of God is contrasted with an acceptance of the cup of being human, down to its last dregs" (Eschatology, Death and Eternal Life, 102).

34. Ferry, *A Brief History of Thought*, 263.

35. Johnny Cash, "1 Corinthians 15:55," in *American VI: Ain't No Grave*, 2010. https://www.youtube.com/watch?v=YP_HjVQII6s

Cited Works

Adams, Marilyn McCord. "Horrendous Evils and the Goodness of God." In *The Problem of Evil*, ed. Marilyn McCord Adams and Robert Merrihew Adams. New York: Oxford University Press, 1990.

———. "Chalcedonian Christology: A Christian Solution to the Problem of Evil." In *Philosophy and Theology Discourse*, ed. Stephen T. Davis. New York: St. Martin's Press, 1997.

———. *Horrendous Evils and the Goodness of God*. Ithaca, NY: Cornell University Press, 1999.

Anscombe, Elizabeth. "What is it to Believe Someone," *Rationality and Religious Belief*, ed. and with introduction C.F. Delaney. Notre Dame, IN: Notre Dame Press, 1979.

Aquinas, Thomas. *Summa Theologiae*, II, II, III. http://www.newadvent.org/summa/.

———. *Faith, Reason and Theology*, Questions 1-4 of his *Commentary on the De Trinitate of Boethius*. Translated by Armand Maurer. Toronto: Pontifical Institute of Medieval Studies, 1987.

———. *The Catechetical Instruction of St. Thomas Aquinas*. Translated by Joseph B. Collins. Manila: Sinag Tala, 1939.

Balthasar, von Hans Urs. *You Crown the Year with Your Goodness*. San Francisco: Ignatius Press, 1989.

Ashley, Benedict. OP. *Living the Truth in Love*. New York: Alba House, 1996.

———. *Choosing a World-View and Value-System: An Ecumenical Apologetics*. New York: Alba House, 2000.

Bavinck, Herman. *Gereformeerde Dogmatiek*, I. Kampen: J.H. Kok, 1895. Edited by John Bolt. Translated by John Vriend as *Reformed*

Dogmatics, Prolegomena, Vol. 1. Grand Rapids, MI: Baker Academic, 2003.

Berkhof, Hendrikus. *Two Hundred Years of Theology*. Translated by John Vriend. Grand Rapids, Michigan: Eerdmans, 1989.

Berkouwer, G.C. *Divine Election*. Translated by Hugo Bekker. Grand Rapids, MI: Eerdmans, 1960.

———. *The Work of Christ*. Translated Cornelius Lambregtse. Grand Rapids, MI: Eerdmans, 1965.

———. *De Heilige Schrift* I-II. Kampen: J.H. Kok, 1966-1967. Translated and edited by Jack B. Rogers as *Holy Scripture*. Grand Rapids, MI: Eerdmans, 1975.

———. "Sacrificium Intellectus?." In *Gereformeerd Theologisch Tijdschrift* 68 (August 1968): 177-200.

———. *Sin*. Translated Philip Holtrop. Grand Rapids, MI: Eerdmans, 1971.

———. "De Achtergrond." In *De Herleving van de Natuurlijke Theologie*. Kampen: J.H. Kok, 1974, 3-17.

———. *Een Halve Eeuw Theologie, Motieven en Stromingen van 1920 to Heden* (Kampen: J.H. Kok, 1974). English Translation: *A Half Century of Theology: Movements and Motives*, translated and edited by Lewis B. Smedes. Grand Rapids, MI: Eerdmans, 1977.

Blocher, Henri. *Original Sin: Illuminating the Riddle*. Grand Rapids: Eerdmans, 1997.

Brownsberger, William. "The Authority of God and the Act of Faith." In *Irish Theological Quarterly*, February 2008 vol. 73, no. 1-2: 148-163.

Bryce, Raymond-Marie, OP, "Does Suffering Lack Meaning? A Contemporary Christian Response." In *New Blackfriars* 98, No. 1076 (July 2017): 436-56.

Calvin, John. *Calvin's Commentaries to the Galatians, Ephesians, Philippians, and Colossians*. Translated T.H.L. Parker, eds. D.W. Torrance, and T. F. Torrance. Grand Rapids, MI: Eerdmans, 1965 [1548].

Catechism of the Catholic Church. http://www.vatican.va/archive/ENG0015/_INDEX.HTM.

Craig, William Lane. "Did Jesus Rise from the Dead?" In *Jesus Under Fire*, Editors, M.J. Wilkins, J. P. Moreland. Grand Rapids, MI: Zondervan, 1995, 142-176.

——. "Dale Allison on Jesus' Empty Tomb, his Postmortem Appearances, and the Origin of the Disciples Belief in his resurrection." In *Philosophia Christi* 10 (2008): 293-301.

——. "God is not Dead Yet," *Christianity Today*, July 2008, 22-27. Online: http://www.reasonablefaith.org/god-is-not-dead-yet.

——. "The New Atheism and Five Arguments for God." Online: http://www.reasonablefaith.org/the-new-atheism-and-five-arguments-for-god.

Davies, Brian, O.P., *Thomas Aquinas on God and Evil*. New York: Oxford University Press, 2011.

Denzinger, Heinrich. *Compendium of Creeds, Definitions, and Declarations on Matters of Faith and Morals*, Latin-English, ed. Peter Hünermann, 43rd Edition, English edition, eds. Robert Fastiggi and Anne Englund Nash. San Francisco: Ignatius Press, 2012.

Dictionary of Biblical Theology, Updated Second Edition, Edited under the Direction of Xavier Léon-Dufour. Translated under the direction of P. Joseph Cahill, S.J. Boston: St. Paul Books & Media, 1995 [1962].

Dooyeweerd, Herman. *Reformation and Scholasticism in Philosophy*. Collected Works, Series A, Volume Three: *Philosophy of Nature and Philosophical Anthropology*. General Editor: D.F.M. Strauss. Translated by Magnus Verbrugge and D.F.M. Strauss. Ancaster, ON: Paideia Press, 2011.

Dulles, Avery Cardinal, S.J. *The Splendor of Faith: The Theological Vision of Pope John Paul II*. New York: Crossroad Publishing Co., 1999.

Dupre, Louis. "Philosophy and the Mystery of Evil." In *Religious Mystery and Rational Reflection*. Grand Rapids, MI: Eerdmans, 1998.

Echeverria, Eduardo. "The Christian faith as a way of life: in appreciation of Francis Schaeffer (on the fiftieth anniversary of L'Abri Fellowship)." In *Evangelical Quarterly* 79, no. 3 (2007): 241-52.

——. *Berkouwer and Catholicism, Disputed Questions*. Leiden/Boston: Brill, 2013.

———. "Revelation and Authority: Preamble of Faith and an Epistemology of Testimony." In *The Fellowship of Catholic Scholar's Quarterly*, Spring/Summer 2014: 18-28.

———. *Pope Francis, The Legacy of Vatican II*. Hobe Sound, FL: Lectio Publishing, 2015.

———. *Divine Election: A Catholic Orientation in Dogmatic and Ecumenical Perspective*. Eugene, OR: Pickwick Publications, 2016.

———. *Revelation, History, and Truth: A Hermeneutics of Dogma*. New York: Peter Lang Publishing, 2017.

Ferry, Luc. *A Brief History of Thought, A Philosophical Guide to Living*. Trans. by Theo Cuffe. New York: Harper Perennial, 2011.

Garcia, J.L.A. "Moral Reasoning & the Catholic Church." In *Oxford Review* (June 1992).

Geach, Peter. *Providence and Evil* (Cambridge: Cambridge University Press, 1977).

Grisez, Germain. *The Way of the Lord Jesus*, vol. 2, *Living a Christian Life*. Quincy, III: Franciscan Press, 1993.

Guinness, Os. *Unspeakable, Facing Up to Evil in an Age of Genocide and Terror*. New York: HarperCollins, 2005.

Gundry, Robert H. *Commentary on the New Testament*. Peabody, MA: Hendrickson Publishers, 2010.

Gutiérrez, Gustavo. *On Job: God-Talk and the Suffering of the Innocent*, trans. Matthew J. O'Connell. Maryknoll, NY: Orbis Books, 1987.

Hart, David Bentley. *The Doors of the Sea, Where was God in the Tsunami?* Grand Rapids, MI: Eerdmans, 2005.

Heidegger, Martin. *Being and Time*, trans. Joan Stambaugh. Albany: State University of New York Press, 1996.

Heidelberg Catechism, 1563. Online: http://www.reformed.org/documents/index.html?mainframe=http://www.reformed.org/documents/heidelberg.html.

Helm, Paul. *The Last Things: Death, Judgment, Heaven, and Hell*. Edinburgh: Banner of Truth Trust, 1989.

———. *Faith and Understanding*. Grand Rapids, MI: Eerdmans, 1997.

———. *Faith, Form, and Fashion*. Eugene: Cascade, 2014.

Hildebrand, Dietrich Von. *Transformation in Christ*. Chicago: Franciscan Herald Press, 1948.

Hooft, van Stan. "The Meaning of Suffering," *Hastings Center Report* 28, no. 5 (1998): 13-19.

James, William. "The Will to Believe" (1896) in *The Will to Believe and other essays in popular philosophy*. New York: Dover Publications, Inc., 1956, 1-31.

John Paul II, *Sign of Contradiction*. Translated by Mary Smith. New York: Crossroad, 1979.

———. *Dives in Misericordia, Rich in Mercy*. Encyclical Letter, 30 November 1980. http://w2.vatican.va/content/john-paul-ii/en/encyclicals/documents/hf_jp-ii_enc_30111980_dives-in-misericordia.html

———. *Salvifici Doloris, On the Christian Meaning of Human Suffering*. Apostolic Letter, 11 February 1984. Online: http://w2.vatican.va/content/john-paul-ii/en/apost_letters/1984/documents/hf_jp-ii_apl_11021984_salvifici-doloris.html.

———. *Veritatis Splendor, The Splendor of Truth*, Encyclical Letter, 6 August 1993.

———. *Crossing the Threshold of Hope*. New York, Knopf. 1995.

———. John Paul II. *A Catechesis on the Creed*, vol. I, *God, Father, and Creator*. Boston: Pauline Books & Media, 1996.

———. *A Catechesis on the Creed*, vol. II, *Jesus, Son and Savior*. Boston: Pauline Books & Media, 1996.

———. *Fides et Ratio, Faith and Reason*. Encyclical Letter, 14 September 1998. Online: http://www.vatican.va/holy_father/john_paul_ii/encyclicals/documents/hf_jp-ii_enc_15101998_fides-et-ratio_en.html.

———. *Novo Millennio Ineunte*. Apostolic Letter. 6 January 2001. http://w2.vatican.va/content/john-paul-ii/en/apost_letters/2001/documents/hf_jp-ii_apl_20010106_novo-millennio-ineunte.html.

———. *Man and Woman He Created Them: A Theology of the Body*. Translated and Introduced by Michael Waldstein. Boston: Pauline

Books & Media, 2006 [1986].

Kalanithi, Paul. *When Breath Becomes Air*. New York: Random House, 2016.

Kang, Y.A. "Levinas on Suffering and Solidarity." In *Tijdschrift voor filosofie* 59, no. 3 (1997): 482-504.

Kasper, Walter Cardinal. *Introduction to Christian Faith*. New York: Paulist Press, 1980.

———. *Mercy, The Essence of the Gospel and the Key to Christian Life*. New York/Mahwah, NJ: Paulist Press, 2013.

Kreeft Peter J., and Ronald K. Tacelli, S.J. *Handbook of Catholic Apologetics, Reasoned Answered to Questions of Faith*. San Francisco: Ignatius Press, 2009.

Levinas, Emmanuel. "Useless Suffering." In *The Provocation of Levinas: Rethinking Other*, ed. Robert Bernasconi and David Wood. New York: Routledge, 1998, 156-67.

Lonergan, Bernard J.F. S.J. *Insight, A Study of Human Understanding*. London: Darton Longman and Todd, 1958.

———. *Method in Theology*. New York: Herder and Herder, 1972.

Mackie, J. L. *The Miracle of Theism*. Oxford: Clarendon Press, 1982.

Maritain, Jacques. *A Preface to Metaphysics*. London: Sheed & Ward, 1945.

———. *On the Grace and Humanity of Jesus*. Translation Joseph W. Evans. New York: Herder and Herder, 1969.

McGrath, Alister E. *Intellectuals Don't Need God & Other Modern Myths*. Grand Rapids, MI: Zondervan Publishing House, 1993.

Marcel, Gabriel. *The Mystery of Being, I, Reflection and Mystery*. Gifford Lectures, 1949-1950. South Bend, IN: St. Augustine, 2001.

McInerny, Ralph. "Philosophizing in Faith." In *Being and Predication*. Washington, D.C.: Catholic University of America Press, 1986.

Morris, Thomas V. *Making Sense of It All, Pascal and the Meaning of Life*. Grand Rapids, MI: Eerdmans, 1992.

Moule, C.F.D. *The Cambridge Greek Testament Commentary: The Epistles to the Colossians and to Philemon*. Cambridge: Cambridge

University Press, 1958.

Mouroux, Jean. *I Believe: The Personal Structure of Faith*. Translated Michael Turner. New York: Sheed and Ward, 1959.

Murray, J. *Redemption—Accomplished and Applied*. Grand Rapids, MI: Eerdmans, 1955.

Newman, John Henry. "Love the Safeguard of Faith Against Superstition," Sermon XII, *Oxford University Sermons*, preached on Whit Sunday (May 21, 1839), http://www.newmanreader.org/works/oxford/serman12.html.

——. Sermon XV, 1843, *Parochial and Plain Sermons*, Vol. I, http://newmanreader.org/works/parochial/volume1/sermon15.html,190-202.

——. *Apologia Pro Vita Sua*. London: J.M. Dent & Sons Ltd., 1864.

Nichols, Aidan, OP. *The Shape of Catholic Theology*. Collegeville, MN: Liturgical Press, 1991.

——. *Epiphany: A Theological Introduction to Catholicism*. Collegeville, Minnesota: The Liturgical Press, 1996.

——. *From Hermes to Benedict XVI: Faith and Reason in Modern Catholic Thought*. Leominster, Herefordshire: Gracewing, 2009.

Oakes, Edward T., S.J. "Original Sin: A Disputation." In *First Things* 87 (November 1998).

O'Collins, Gerald, S.J. and Farrugia, Edward G. Editors. *A Concise Dictionary of Theology*. New York: Paulist Press, 1991.

Olson, Roger E. "A Crucial but Much Ignored (or Misunderstood) Distinction for Theology: 'Mystery' versus 'Contradiction'." February 10, 2016. Online: http://www.patheos.com/blogs/rogereolson/2016/02/a-crucial-but-much-ignored-or-misunderstood-distinction-for-theology-mystery-versus-contradiction/.

Orr, James. *God's Image in Man and Its Defacement in the Light of Modern Denials*, 1903-1904 Stone Lectures, Princeton Theological Seminary. Grand Rapids: Eerdmans, 1948.

Pope Francis. *The Name of God is Mercy*. New York, Random House. 2016.

——. *Misericordiae Vultus*. Bull of Indiction of the Extraordinary

Jubilee of Mercy. https://w2.vatican.va/content/francesco/en/apost_
letters/documents/papa-francesco_bolla_20150411_misericordiae-
vultus.html.

Plantinga, Alvin. *Warranted Christian Belief.* Oxford: Oxford University Press, 2000.

Rahner, Karl and Herbert Vorgrimler. *Theological Dictionary.* Editor,
Cornelius Ernst, O.P. Translated by Richard Strachan. New York:
Herder & Herder, 1965.

Ratzinger, Joseph. *Eschatology, Death and Eternal Life.* Translated Michael Waldstein; Translated and edited, Aidan Nichols, O.P. Washington, D.C.: The Catholic University of America Press, 1988.

——. *Introduction to Christianity.* Translated J.R. Foster. San Francisco: Ignatius, 1990 [1968].

——. *The Yes of Jesus Christ.* Translated Robert Nowell. New York:
Crossroad, 1991.

——. *The Nature and Mission of Theology.* Translated Adrian Walker.
San Francisco: Ignatius Press, 1995.

——. *Truth and Tolerance: Christian Belief and World Religions.* Translated Henry Taylor. San Francisco: Ignatius Press, 2004.

——. *Christianity and the Crisis of Cultures.* Translated Brian McNeil.
San Francisco: Ignatius Press, 2006.

——. *Dogma and Preaching, Applying Christian Doctrine to Daily Life.*
Translated Michael J. Miller and Matthew J. O'Connell, ed. Michael
J. Miller. San Francisco: Ignatius Press, 2011.

Rogers, Patrick V., C.P. *Colossians.* Wilmington, Delaware: Michael
Glazier, Inc. 1980.

Routledge Encyclopedia of Philosophy. Editor, Edward Craig. London:
Routledge, 1998.

Rowe, William, L. "Evil and the Theistic Hypothesis: A Response to
Wykstra." In *The Problem of Evil,* ed. Marilyn McCord Adams and
Robert Merrihew Adams. New York: Oxford University Press, 1990.

Russell, Bertrand. "A Free Man's Worship," (1903). In *The Meaning
of Life,* ed. E.D. Klemke. New York: Oxford University Press, 1981,
55-62

Sacramentum Verbi. An Encyclopedia of Biblical Theology. Edited by Johannes B. Bauer, Volume 3. New York: Herder and Herder, 1970.

Saward, John "Christ The Light of the Nations, Part I." Online: http://christendom-awake.org/pages/jsaward/lightofnations1.htm.

———. *Christ Is the Answer: The Christ-Centered Teaching of John Paul II.* New York: Alba House, 1995.

Schaeffer, Francis A. *The God Who is There.* Downers Grove, IL: Inter-Varsity Press, 1968.

———. *He Is There and He Is Not Silent.* London: Hodder and Stoughton, 1972.

———. *The Finished Work of Christ: The Truth of Romans 1-8.* Wheaton, Ill.: Crossway Books, 1998.

———. *True Spirituality*, 30th Anniversary Edition. Wheaton, IL: Tyndale House Publishers 2001.

Schweizer, Eduard. *The Letter to the Colossians: A Commentary.* Minneapolis, Minn.: Augsburg, 1982.

Sproul, R.C. *Chosen by God.* Wheaton, IL: Tyndale, 1986.

Stott, John R.W. *The Cross of Christ.* Downers Grove, Illinois: IVP Books, 2006 (1986).

Stump, Eleonore. "Aquinas on the Sufferings of Job." In *The Evidential Argument from Evil*, ed. Daniel Howard-Synder. Bloomington, Ind.: Indiana University Press, 1996, 49-68.

Swinburne, Richard. *Faith and Reason.* Oxford: Clarendon Press, 1981.

Taylor, Charles. *Varieties of Religion Today: William James Revisited.* Cambridge, MA: Harvard University Press, 2002.

Trigg, Roger. "Can a Religion Rest on Historical Claims." *Rationality and Religion.* Oxford: Blackwell, 1998, 91-112

Vanhoozer, Kevin. "Hermeneutics of I-Witness Testimony." In *First Theology: God, Scriptures and Hermeneutics.* Downers Grove, IL: Inter-Varsity Press; Leicester: Apollos, 2002.

———. *Biblical Authority After Babel.* Grand Rapids, MI: Brazos Press, 2016.

Vatican II, *Gaudium et spes*. Online: http://www.vatican.va/archive/ hist_councils/ii_vatican_council/documents/vat-ii_cons_19651207_ gaudium-et-spes_en.html.

Wahlberg, Mats. *Revelation as Testimony, A Philosophical-Theological Study*. Grand Rapids, MI: Eerdmans, 2014.

Weinandy, Thomas. OFM Cap., *Does God Suffer?* Notre Dame: University of Notre Dame Press, 2000.

White, Thomas Joseph, OP. *The Light of Christ, An Introduction to Catholicism*. Washington, DC: The Catholic University of America Press, 2017.

Wolterstorff, Nicholas. *Lament for a Son*. Grand Rapids: Eerdmans, 1987.

Wright, N. T. *Evil and the Justice of God*. Downers Grove, IL: IVP Books, 2006.

Zagzebski, Linda. "A Modern Defense of Religious Authority." In *Logos*, Vol. 19, 3 (2016).

Index

Adams, Marilyn McCord, 61, 90n27,

Agnosticism, 16-21

    see also William James

Anscombe, Elizabeth, 22, 44n17

Aquinas, Thomas, 13, 26, 40, 44n16, 58, 129n28

Ashley, Benedict, OP, 62-63, 79, 82-83, 91n31, 99, 103-104

Assertoric authority, 23

Augustine, 122-23

Balthasar, Hans Urs von, 101

Berkouwer, G.C. 27-43, 74-75, 88n6, 88n9

    see also Revelation and authority, 27-43

Berger, Peter, 8

Berkhof, Hendrikus, 46n57

Bonhoeffer, Dietrich, 35-36, 46n57

    See also positivism of revelation, 35-36

Cash, Johnny, 127-28

Catechism of the Catholic Church, 3, 6, 9, 56, 60, 62, 71, 72, 77, 79, 81, 87n2, 96, 108n16, 113-14, 118, 121-122, 123-24

Chalcedonian Christology, 84, 90n27, 91n28

Christian Anthropology, 121, 129n27

Craig, William Lane, 43n3, 45n39

Deely, Genevieve, Foreword

Davies, Brian, OP, 52-53, 60

Dulles, Avery, 105

Dupre, Louis, 9-10, 49, 50

Echeverria, Eduardo, 43n9, 45n34, 88n5, 108n5, 129n17

Expanded Theism, 69n27

Faith, 25-27

    see also revelation and authority, 27-43

CPSIA information can be obtained
at www.ICGtesting.com
Printed in the USA
LVOW10s0258220318
570733LV00001B/1/P